Making Money
from Holiday Lets

Making Money from Holiday Lets

A start-up handbook for buying and letting holiday homes

JACKIE TAYLOR

How To Books

Published by How To Books Ltd,
3 Newtec Place, Magdalen Road,
Oxford, OX4 1RE, United Kingdom.
Tel: (01865) 793806.   Fax: (01865) 248780.
info@howtobooks.co.uk
www.howtobooks.co.uk

First edition 2001

British Library Cataloguing in Publication Data
A catalogue record for this book is available from
the British Library.

Edited by Peter Williams
Cartoons by Mike Flanagan
Cover design by Shireen Nathoo Design
Cover image PhotoDisc

Produced for How To Books by Deer Park Productions
Typeset by Anneset, Weston-super-Mare, North Somerset
Printed and bound by Cromwell Press, Trowbridge, Wiltshire

Note: The material contained in this book is set out in good
faith for general guidance and no liability can be accepted
for loss or expense incurred as a result of relying in particular
circumstances on statements made in the book. The laws and
regulations are complex and liable to change, and readers should
check the current position with the relevant authorities before
making personal arrangements.

Contents

List of Illustrations

Preface

Have you ever thought about making money from holiday lets? Perhaps you have an old barn that could be converted, or you want to move to the country and are looking for a small business you can run yourself? Whether you are planning a complex of cottages or a single holiday flat, this book will help you make a success of your venture.

It is intended as a practical guide to the whole range of subjects you'll need to think about if you want to run a successful holiday let business. It covers finding and buying a property, converting existing buildings, preparing for guests, effective marketing and advertising plus keeping on top of finances and the day-to-day running of your business.

It includes case studies and practical exercises – checklists, self-assessment questionnaires and worked examples – all designed to help you start off on the right track.

I hope that if you have a dream of running a holiday let business, this book will give you the knowledge and the confidence you need to get started. The book is dedicated to my husband, Peter; we dreamed of moving to the country and running a holiday cottage business. We did it – and so can you!

Jackie Taylor

1

Getting Started

A holiday let business can:

- provide additional income, making use of an existing granny flat or annex or perhaps involving the conversion of redundant buildings;

- provide an investment opportunity, with the objective of earning income and achieving capital growth over a number of years;

- be seen as a semi-retirement or 'lifestyle' option for someone looking for a change of pace.

Holiday let businesses range from individual holiday cottages through to multiple unit chalet sites, from properties with no facilities to those with bars, entertainment and shops. There is no typical holiday let. But it is true to say that although there are some large operations, in general, holiday let businesses are small-scale and owner-managed. Many people go into holiday lets with no previous experience in tourism, except as customers. And, in common with many small businesses, the failure rate is high.

The key is preparation: researching the business you're going into, understanding the economics of what you're doing and having the drive and determination to achieve success.

DECIDING ON HOLIDAY LETS

Holiday lets can provide extra income with relatively little work, but some of the realities are:

- a small financial return compared to the capital cost of holiday property;

- no steady cash flow;

- if you manage cleaning, maintenance and bookings yourself, less flexibility than you might think – for example, someone needs to be available year-round to deal with enquiries.

Having said all of that, you will be getting huge satisfaction from running all aspects of a business yourself and gaining control of your own working life. You will probably find that many guests become more like friends, returning year after year. Although you may get the odd difficult or careless guest, these should be a very small minority; in general, the more care that you take in cleaning and presenting your holiday lets, the more care people will take of them.

Before deciding on holiday lets, alternatives you might want to consider are:

- running a bed and breakfast or a guest house; or

- going into longer term residential letting.

Comparing self-catering and B&B

Advantages of self-catering:

- people look after themselves – no cooking;

- cleaning only after each letting period;

- most holidays are pre-booked – you are not reliant on passing trade and cash flow can be evened out with the taking of deposits in advance;

- self-catering is easily combined with other work or activities – apart from meeting and greeting, you can plan your time to suit yourself.

On the negative side, the financial rewards are slim, your cash is tied up in property and you may have to work harder at maintenance than you think.

Comparing holiday lets and tenancies

Instead of utilising a property for holiday lets, you may wish to consider offering the property as a residential let.

Holiday lets	**Tenants**
● Higher rents, shorter season	● Lower rent but regular and year round
● Advertising and marketing costs can be very expensive for a single unit	● One-off advertising cost for each new tenant
● More work – weekly cleaning	● Cleaning only at end of tenancy and maintenance as required
● Don't know who your guests will be, how noisy for example	● Some control over who you take as a tenant. Can interview them, take up references
● Must be furnished and equipped	● Could be furnished or unfurnished
● Guests only in place for a week or two	● Tenants around for longer – so a good relationship with your tenant is helpful

Looking at types of holiday lets

There are various types of holiday lets:

● single or multiple units;
● managed by an agency, by a manager or by the owner;
● attached to an existing property or self-contained;
● dedicated to holiday use or used for a mix of holiday and winter lets;
● designed for holidays or an ordinary residential property.

Arm's length lets

It is possible to run a holiday let at arm's length, employing an agent to deal with bookings and arranging for someone locally to cover cleaning and maintenance. This is a popular option, particularly where the building has been bought for investment or as a future retirement home; the property effectively is made to pay for itself until it is either sold or utilised for the family.

Advantages:

- little work involved;

- income helps to offset the costs of keeping the property.

Disadvantages:

- lack of control – over guests, over quality of cleaning and maintenance;

- this is not a way to make money – paying for others to do the work equals higher costs.

Owner management

You may choose to manage your holiday let yourself.

Advantages:

- control over quality – of cleaning, maintenance and general customer care;

- it is cheaper – you are not paying someone to do the work for you;

- you still have the option of using an agent for bookings if you prefer.

Disadvantages:

- your changeover day will be tied up every week that you have guests;

- you will be limited when you can take your own holidays, particularly in the summer and during other school holidays;

- if handling bookings yourself, your ability to get away even during the winter months will be limited unless you make other arrangements. You may be closed to guests during the winter, but January and February will be your peak time for taking enquiries and bookings.

Employing a manager

The profitability of holiday lets is low, and in general it is only the larger establishments in this sector that would generate sufficient funds to enable a manager to be employed.

Mixing holiday and winter lets

One way of maximising income is to use the property as a holiday let during the peak summer season, then to let it out to a tenant over the winter. It is very important here to check planning consents: properties may be designated solely as holiday properties with rental restricted to a certain number of months per year.

You will also need to consider whether your property is suitably heated and ventilated for occupation during the winter. Wear and tear during the winter months can be high; don't forget to schedule time between the end of the let and the start of the holiday season for decoration and maintenance.

Advantages

● maximises income potential;

● property is occupied and heated throughout the winter.

Disadvantages

● property must have residential consent;

● depending on the area, it can be difficult to find a tenant requiring furnished accommodation for just a few months, particularly where a number of holiday homes come onto the ordinary letting market at the end of the summer.

Letting out part of your house

This could be part of a house that has been subdivided, an adjoining granny annex or flat, or a building in the garden or grounds.

It is worth mentioning here that people on holiday can be demanding of your time; many holidaymakers feel that chatting to the owners is an integral part of their holiday. They may well want to talk to you about their day or come knocking on the door at night to borrow milk – depending on the location of the let in relation to the house, this may not be the best option for people who enjoy their own privacy.

IDENTIFYING YOUR PERSONAL OBJECTIVES

It is very helpful if you can clarify your objectives before you start any conversion work or start to invest any time in searching for a property.

Some questions to consider

● How much time do you want to spend running the business?

● How much of the work do you want to do yourselves and how much do you want to 'buy in'?

● What sort of lifestyle do you see yourselves having?

● How much risk are you willing to take in this venture?

● What level of income do you want?

● How much work are you expecting other members of the family to put in?

It might be helpful if each member of the family sits down and thinks about these questions, particularly in terms of how this new business venture will affect their lifestyle. Looking at everyone's expectations at an early stage will help minimise problems later on. For example, do your children know that you're expecting them to clean every Saturday through the summer, for free, until you get the business started? And do they understand that you won't be able to go away in the summer holidays?

You should also make sure that everyone's expectations are realistic. If you decide that you want to spend roughly three days per week working on your holiday lets, will this conflict with your dream of developing and maintaining twenty acres of formal gardens around your new home? An extreme example, but it illustrates the point that you should clarify these issues in advance of making any decisions.

ASSESSING YOUR SKILLS

Running your own business

Starting up and running your own business demands commitment, drive and self-motivation. In the holiday let business, you are most likely to succeed if you:

● like people;

● genuinely want people to enjoy their holiday and are prepared to put in that extra effort to ensure that they do so;

● have a flexible approach;

● are practical and skilled in a number of areas.

While it is possible to run your business completely at arm's length, most successful holiday lets are generally run by people who are prepared to put in that extra effort in welcoming and caring for their guests, from polite, efficient service when dealing with bookings to provision of little extra touches like tea and coffee on arrival.

Practical skills

The more skills you have, the more likely you are to keep costs to a minimum. Not all the skills in Figure 1 will be applicable to your type of business, but if they are, consider whether this is a skill that you or your family have, whether it is something you can learn or whether it is something you will have to look to other people to provide.

Obviously, the standard of work in a holiday let has to be high, and where safety issues are involved, for example with electrical wiring, then you should get a professional to undertake the work.

PLANNING YOUR NEW VENTURE

This section looks at some of the other issues you need to consider before you commit yourself to a holiday let business.

Moving to a new area

If you are moving to a new area, think hard about:

● the impact on your spouse and/or family;

● the potential sense of isolation and lack of social contact you may experience initially;

● the stress of moving combined with the stress of a new venture;

Skill Area	Is it needed in your business?	Do you have this skill?	Can you learn this skill?	Will you have to pay someone to do this work?
Maintenance				
Plumbing				
Electrical work				
Painting				
Building				
Joinery				
Bricklaying				
Cleaning				
Gardening				
Marketing				
Advertising				
Brochures				
Pricing				
Administration				
Bookings				
Keeping records				
Letter writing				
Book-keeping				
PAYE/NICs/VAT				
Budgeting				
Hiring staff				
Supervising staff				
Staff salaries				
Computer skills				
Word processing				
Spreadsheets				
E-mail				
Website production				
Other				
Customer relations				

Fig. 1. A skills self-assessment.

- how your children will cope with a new school and making new friends;

- the lack of local knowledge – and no support network to help you.

The stress of starting a new business

This will be an extremely exciting time, but it will also be extremely demanding. It is very likely that everything will be new to you and you will be on a steep learning curve. Do you enjoy a challenge? How will you cope under pressure?

Working with your family

Many holiday lets are run by couples. Working together is bound to put stresses and strains on even the happiest of relationships. Although most decisions will be jointly and amicably made, it may be prudent to list the functions of the business and to decide which of you has the final say in each area (see Figure 2).

Business area	Who has the lead responsibility?
Marketing and advertising	
Customer relations	
Accounts and financial control	
Staff hiring and supervision	
Interior furnishings and inventory	
Interior maintenance	
Exterior maintenance	
Landscaping and grounds	
Cleaning	

Fig. 2. Defining responsibilities.

CASE STUDIES

Throughout the book, we will return to one couple and two individuals who are starting different types of holiday let businesses.

Fiona and Michael want to escape the rat race

Fiona and Michael are in their late forties with children who have left home. Michael is an engineer who has taken early retirement. Fiona is a teacher but she feels ready for a change of direction and would like to run her own business. They want to move near to the sea and are considering selling their house in London and using Michael's lump sum either to buy an existing business or to buy a property to convert into a holiday cottage complex.

Sue wants to earn some extra income

Sue is a nurse in her thirties living in a seaside resort. The granny flat attached to her house hasn't been occupied since she moved in, and she is considering letting it out to holidaymakers during the height of the summer season in order to earn some money from it. The flat will need some work and Sue is wondering whether it will be worth her while.

George wants to make the most of his property

George has a smallholding in a very quiet part of the countryside that is popular with hikers. He has recently inherited some money and is wondering whether to use it to convert one of his outbuildings to a holiday cottage. He is a practical person and believes that he can keep costs to a minimum by doing most of the work himself. When the project is finished, he hopes that he will earn some extra income year-round and increase the value of his smallholding in the process.

CHECKLIST

- Take time to review whether you really want to be involved in the holiday let business.

- Start to think about what type of holiday let will be best for you.

- Ensure that you and your family have realistic expectations of what is involved.

- Review your skills against what is going to be required. Organise training or development where necessary.

2

Researching the Market

The scope of your initial market research will depend on the size of your business. It may be sensible to let out your annex and see how it goes without doing very much research at all. But if you intend to derive a significant percentage of your household income from the business, or if you intend to invest substantial sums buying or renovating a property, you need to make sure that you get it right. Time consuming though it is, thorough research at the outset will pay dividends later on.

The objective of this research is to start to formulate the sort of business you will be running and to plan for success. The key stages in the process are:

● *Researching the market* – what are the prospects for your business?

● *Finding the right location* – what is it about your chosen location that will attract guests?

● *Understanding what people want* – what level of service and facilities do your target customers expect?

● *Analysing the competition* – what are you up against?

IDENTIFYING THE MARKET

Researching market trends

You will need to ensure that the prospects for your type of holiday let in your specific area are good. Places to start your market research are:

● local tourism trade associations;

● regional tourist boards;

- local and district council tourism and economic development offices;

- local development agencies.

The sort of information you should be looking for is:

- whether tourism in the area is in growth or in decline;

- which sectors of the market are performing well or performing badly;

- which locations experience the strongest demand for accommodation;

- whether there is an over- or under-supply of accommodation in any particular area or sector of the market;

- whether there is any assistance available for new tourism businesses in the area.

CASE STUDY

Fiona and Michael pick a location

Fiona and Michael have started to look at properties but are finding that places near to the sea fall outside their price range. They identify an area inland close to several interesting towns and historic houses where they would like to live themselves. Initially they are worried that the distance from the sea will limit the number of potential guests, but they meet with the regional tourist office and come away with information that the area has a strong attraction for people looking for heritage breaks, that the number of historic buildings in the area is a strong draw for overseas visitors, and that these sectors of the market are very fast growing and provide an extended, year-round season.

They therefore decide to look for a property with a view to targeting the top end of the market, primarily older couples and overseas visitors with an interest in heritage, history, antiques, etc.

Looking into the future

As well as looking at past performance, you will need to consider trends that are emerging now which will impact on the future of your business. Recent developments include:

● growth in short breaks and out-of-season holidays;

● growth in activity-based and learning holidays;

● the grey pound – growth in the retirement market;

● an increasing interest in 'green' issues and sustainable tourism;

● a general trend towards higher standards in the self-catering industry;

● the rapid growth of holiday bookings via the Internet.

Looking at economic trends

You will need to consider how the general state of the economy may impact on your business.

Strength of sterling
For both British and overseas visitors, the strength of the pound will impact on the attractiveness of a UK-based holiday compared to other destinations.

General economic climate
The impact of the economy may not be obvious. During recessions, will people take less overseas holidays, thus strengthening the UK holiday market? Or will they stop spending on holidays altogether? Certainly, value for money will become an even more important consideration. In times of relative prosperity, will more people take overseas holidays? Or will there be a positive impact on the UK sector as people take longer holidays, or more second holidays and winter breaks?

Identifying your customers

You will need to build up a profile of the type of person who will spend their holiday with you. You will probably have more than one profile: for example, most of your summer visitors may be families with school-age children looking for a beach holiday, while out of season, the majority of your guests may be professional or retired couples taking a short break.

It may be helpful to picture these people. Is there a family you know that fits your idea of your target customer? If there is, keep them in mind. Marketing is all about understanding what your customer wants and then providing it. A clear picture of your target customer will help you do this.

Who are your customers?

● Age, family group, interests, occupations.

● Where are they from:
  – the UK – which parts?
  – overseas – which countries?

Why do they choose a self-catering holiday?
A major factor is the freedom for guests to come and go on their own terms. Price is also a factor – holiday lets are a cheaper option than serviced accommodation. Guests may also enjoy a home-from-home atmosphere or eating out in different restaurants.

What do they enjoy doing on holiday?
A whole range of possibilities, including relaxing, going to the beach, walking, shopping, eating out, cycling, horse riding, swimming, playing tennis, golf, visiting stately homes, gardens and theme parks.

How many holidays to they take each year?

● Will this be their main holiday?

● Or a second holiday, or an off-season break?

● If a second holiday, what is their main holiday destination?

● When do they take their holidays?

● Are they likely to return to your accommodation in following years?

● How price sensitive are they likely to be?

● How do they choose a holiday and who makes the decisions?

Although you may not be able to answer all these questions exactly, you should be able to build a general profile of the type of visitor you will

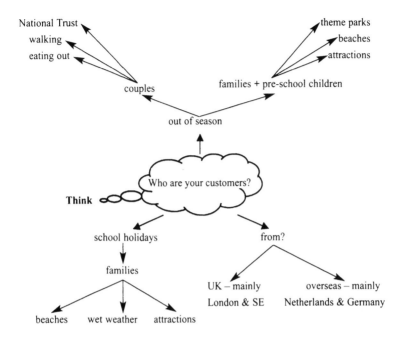

National Trust
walking
eating out

theme parks
beaches
attractions

couples   families + pre-school children

out of season

Think Who are your customers?

school holidays   from?

families

UK – mainly   overseas – mainly
London & SE   Netherlands & Germany

beaches   wet weather   attractions

Fig. 3.   An example of a mind map®

be targeting. You may find a mind map a useful tool in starting to build this profile (see Figure 3).

SELECTING THE RIGHT LOCATION

Buildings can be changed, facilities upgraded, gardens landscaped, but you can do little if the location of your business is unfavourable. The location of your holiday let will directly impact on your occupancy rates which in turn will impact directly on your income.

Inevitably, location will be a major factor in the price you have to pay for a property. A cottage with a sea view will cost far more than the equivalent property inland. On the other hand, it will also be more sought after as a holiday let and will command a higher rental: in the end, getting the location right will be a balancing act between what you can afford and the income you need to generate.

If you are looking to move to a new area, you will need to consider:

● whether the area meets the needs of you and your family; and

- whether it is a good location for your business.

Getting it right for you and your family

You will need to be very clear about the requirements of all family members. Some points to consider are as follows:

- Proximity to supermarkets and other shops.

- Schools and colleges – their quality and location.

- Transport – do any of your family need access to public transport? If you are planning to move to a rural area, this can be a major problem. Where are the nearest bus, coach and train services? How good are the roads? How easy is it to connect to the motorway network?

- Proximity to entertainment, sporting facilities, restaurants. Do you have any special interests or hobbies and can you take part in them in this location? What is the social life like in the area and will it suit you?

- How many of the local facilities stay open in the winter? This is particularly important if you are considering moving to a tourist area where there is a great difference between life in and out of the holiday season.

- Availability of jobs – if you or a member of your family needs to work, are there suitable, year-round opportunities in the area?

Getting it right for your visitors

Key questions are:

- what's special about this place?

- who would want to holiday here? and

- does this coincide with the type of business you want to be in?

There will be some overlap between the facilities that you and your family need and the facilities your customers need, for example supermarkets, restaurants, sports facilities. In addition, you will need to think about:

Existing and planned visitor attractions
What will people do when the weather is bad? Which attractions are open all year round? How close are beaches, moorland, countryside, historic towns?

Opportunities for activity or sporting holidays
Is the area good for walking, cycling, horse riding, surfing, sailing, etc.?

What is the typical length of the season in the area?
As a broad indicator, the further south in England, the longer the season. But historic towns may attract visitors all year round.

Is the area well known for any particular craft or occupation?
For example pottery, antiques, mining – you are looking for something that gives the area a unique flavour which can be used to market your accommodation.

Has the area had any links with authors or books or famous historical figures?
For example Poldark country, Brontë country – again, you are looking for a marketing angle.

Are any festivals or events held in the area?
Music, art and cultural festivals, traditional events – all will help you sell the area as a holiday destination.

Can people reach the area easily?
Again there will be a cost/income trade-off here, with property in remote areas costing less but enjoying lower occupancy rates.

What is the general attitude to tourism in the area?
This is particularly relevant if you think you may need planning permission to convert buildings, extend facilities or change access. Even if you don't have a specific site in mind, an informal discussion with local planning officers will be invaluable.

Other businesses in the area
Off-season company lets can be a good source of income, with many

people preferring the flexibility of self-catering to staying in a guest-house or hotel. Local colleges often need accommodation for people on short courses. Any opportunities to extend the length of your season are worth investigating.

UNDERSTANDING WHAT PEOPLE WANT

Think about your target customers. You have an idea now of who they are. Your job as the operator of a holiday letting business is to provide these customers with what they want at a price they are willing to pay.

The main ways of finding out what customers expect are:

● asking friends, colleagues or family who represent your customer profile what they would expect from a holiday let;

● looking at the competition: examining what your competitors offer to see what the industry standard is and how you can better it;

● once you are in business, asking your customers, either informally or through surveys. They are the best source of information you can access.

CASE STUDY

George reworks his costings

George arranges to meet a specialist farm holiday agency before he even begins work on his conversion. They suggest that if he wants to attract people year-round, then he should give more thought in his plans to heating than he has already, and that he should also consider providing laundry and drying facilities.

They also discuss parking and access, which is currently over a very rough farm track. The agency thinks that it will not be acceptable for guests. George had planned to upgrade the access after he had some money coming in from lettings. He realises that he will have to do more work to bring his property up to a reasonable standard for holiday letting than he had originally thought. He starts to rework his costings to take into account the extra expenses.

Furnishing and equipping your lets

Standards in the self-catering industry are rising every year. Inevitably, there will be a trade-off between cost and level of facilities – the key is matching the accommodation to the customer. Families with children may be looking for a reasonably priced summer holiday. They may well be less concerned about coordinating curtains and linen than the availability of indoor activities to amuse the children if the weather is bad. On the other hand, if you are targeting older, more affluent couples for your chocolate-box country cottage, then the quality of furniture and furnishings will be very important.

There are certain things that you must provide:

● accommodation that meets all health and safety and other legal requirements (see Chapter 8);

● accommodation that is well-maintained and spotlessly clean;

● accommodation that is perceived as providing good value for money, whether at the top or bottom end of the market;

● good, clear information about your accommodation and the facilities and services in the local area.

Inventories will be discussed later in this book. But at the initial planning and research stage, you need to think about the quality and level of equipment and furnishings, for example:

Quality of interiors
Quality of furniture, soft furnishings, interior decoration, linen, etc.

Provision of equipment
Over and above the basic level of equipment, will you provide additional kitchen items (coffee makers, microwaves, etc.), freezers, dishwashers, washing machines, TVs in bedrooms, videos, radios?

Quality of site
Manicured lawns or wildlife garden? Facilities for children, dog walking areas, provision for parking.

Extra facilities
Games rooms, indoor and outdoor sports activities, laundry, telephone facilities.

Extra services

Will your customers expect a meal or bar service, entertainment, an initial grocery delivery, babysitting or daily milk and newspapers, for example?

LOOKING AT THE COMPETITION

Your competitors will be one of your best sources of information. You need to understand what the standard offering is for the type of business you're operating. You need to understand what the successful operators are doing well and what less successful operators are doing wrong. All the time, you should be looking for good ideas and thinking about what is different about your operation that you can use to build a successful business.

Becoming a customer

Stay in as many places that are similar to your proposed business as you can. Look critically at each one. Why did you pick a particular cottage? How are the owners targeting their potential customers? How are the units equipped? What are they offering both inside and outside the units? What worked well? What would you do differently? Make notes and keep them.

Request brochures for similar properties in your target area. Compare what they offer and what they are charging.

Above all, talk to the operators: they are the people with first-hand knowledge of the realities of the business.

Talking to agencies

Look at agency brochures for the range of accommodation offered, particularly in your area. Facilities will be listed and there are often pictures of both exteriors and interiors. Agencies will also supply information to potential property owners regarding what they would expect to see in any property that they represent.

Surfing the Internet

Details of many holiday properties are now published on the Internet. While some sites have very basic information, others have much more detailed descriptions and photographs of the accommodation on offer.

CASE STUDY

Sue has to think again

Sue decides that she will try to rent out her flat for the summer season only. She will aim her accommodation at families, offering clean but basic accommodation. The flat has two bedrooms and she thinks that she will be able to accommodate up to six people with one double bedroom, one small bedroom with bunk beds and a sofa bed in the living area, and on this basis, she calculates that her potential income will be quite reasonable.

She knows several people in the town who rent out holiday flats and as she starts to talk to them, she is surprised to hear that they find it difficult to fill their accommodation, even in the summer. It seems that there is a glut of reasonably priced, family accommodation in the town and that the market appears to be in decline, with families preferring to stay in out-of-town holiday parks with a wide range of facilities and entertainment programmes. She decides to think again about what she can offer to visitors that will differentiate her accommodation from the competition in the town.

CHECKLIST

- Research which sectors of the market are performing well.

- Understand what sort of customers you will be aiming for.

- Understand what these customers expect.

- Start to plan how you will meet their expectations.

3

Finding the Right Property

In this chapter, we will look at purchasing a property, some of the considerations involved in buying a going concern and, finally, renovating a property.

LOOKING FOR A PROPERTY

Sources of information include:

- national newspapers, especially Sunday supplements;

- local newspapers in the area you want to buy – if this is a daily paper, find out when their business and property sections appear;

- *Dalton's Weekly*, self-build magazines (for barns etc. to convert), smallholders' magazines, etc.;

- estate agents;

- business transfer agents;

- specialist tourism and leisure industry agents;

- the Internet;

- local tourism associations are always worth a call – they'll know what's for sale in their area;

- regional tourism boards – who should keep lists of agents specialising in holiday homes.

Before you start

Talking to estate agents
Spend some time talking to agents. Get a view as to whether there is much property available and at what sort of price range, whether there is less or more available than previously and what in their opinion is the best time to be looking.

Timing
If you are viewing going concerns, you should be looking in the off-peak season. Your access to units already let in the high season is going to be quite limited. If possible, try to view the property in all weathers.

What are you looking for?
Before you start looking, think about what you want – the 'must haves' – and make a list of your criteria.

PREPARING TO VIEW

Viewing a property is very time-consuming, both for yourself and for the current owners. Although you may want to look at everything that's available, it is much more likely that you will need to prepare a shortlist.

Before you go

Talk to the agent about the property or business and get their views, while bearing in mind that it is their job to sell the property. Talk to someone who actually knows the property – this could well save you time further along. Try to find out:

● how long it has been on the market;

● how much interest there has been in the property;

● whether it is or has been previously under offer;

● why the owners are selling.

At this stage, clarify anything in the particulars that you don't understand. Look for omissions – is there anything that hasn't been said?

If you aren't familiar with the area, try to do some investigations first. Look at the position of the property on an Ordinance Survey map. If possible, drive around the area before you arrange an appointment to visit.

During your visit

Viewing properties can be confusing, particularly if you're viewing several properties in a short space of time. You will probably find that when you start to think about the property after the event, you will have completely forgotten some things. It's vital that you make some sort of record, either during or immediately after your visits.

- Draw a plan of the property, covering the overall layout and a plan of each unit.

- Perhaps take photos if you are particularly interested in a property (having asked the owner's permission first).

- Ask for some time to go around the property on your own, probably after you've been given a tour by the owner – that way you are more likely to take in what you are seeing and have a better understanding of the basic layout and features of the property.

The sort of information you'll be looking to collect will depend on the type of property you're viewing, but basically you will be looking at things such as:

First impressions
Try to take note of your first impressions of a property. Think about how a guest will react on seeing your property for the first time. Is the access good, the entrance welcoming, the external appearance attractive – and if not, could it be made so?

The site and buildings

- Basic layout of site – buildings and rooms within buildings, storage, gardens and grounds.

- Services – electricity, mains or bottled gas, type of heating, mains or private water supply, mains or private drainage.

- General state of internal and external repair. State of existing fixtures and fittings, furnishings. Potential ease of maintenance.

- State of the access to the site. Rights of way. Location and state of boundaries and fencing. Parking. If there is private, shared access, what are the arrangements for upkeep?

- Existing facilities – for example, laundry, children's play areas, animal shelters, tennis courts, etc.

- Local conditions: for example, proximity to mine workings.

The business

- How long have the present owners been at the property?

- What work have they carried out?

- Why are they selling? (Be aware that the answer you receive may not be the true one.)

- How many weeks' bookings do they achieve? Do they open all year round? What is their level of repeat bookings?

- How many bookings do they have for the coming season?

- Where do they advertise? Where do most bookings come from?

The location

- What existing consents are in place, for example for residential or holiday use? Are there any limitations on months of trading?

- What planning permissions are current, lapsed or submitted but turned down?

- Are there any constraints placed by the situation, for example within a National Park?

- How close are the nearest neighbours? How do they view holiday lets? Have there been any disputes with the neighbours?

The accounts
It is not normal practice for the accounts of the business to be made available to a prospective buyer until after a property has been viewed, perhaps for a second time. What you will eventually see will usually be an extract from the accounts, excluding items such as finance charges which will vary from person to person depending on the level of borrowings.

A trading history over several years is extremely useful. Is the trend upward or downward for turnover and for profits? The first things to look for are changes year on year: can the owner explain these?

Key figures you'll be looking for are:

● turnover;

● business rates, where applicable – these will be a major expense;

● utility bills – gas, electric, water, telephone;

● advertising costs – and how these break down between types of advertising, different publications, etc.;

● staff costs;

● cleaning and laundry costs;

● other expenses, with some idea of how these break down into items such as consumables, repairs, replacements and so on.

Where there are value-added services, for example a bar or meal service, the income and costs should be separately identified.

The purchase price
You will need to discuss exactly what is and what is not included in the purchase price, particularly whether any of the items currently in the units are not included in the price, and whether there is any stock to be carried over and paid for separately.

Before you leave, ask for copies of the current brochure, promotional material and tariffs.

Buying into a successful business

The current success or otherwise of an establishment is one of the key areas that you will need to assess during a visit. Not only will this impact on the asking price, but it will also be a significant factor in analysing future income and profit levels.

For a business trading close to its limits:

● success will be reflected in the asking price;

● you will have the advantage of a good basis on which to forecast your income;

● you will have little work to do to bring the business up to its potential;

● but there may be an initial drop in business when you take over.

Many people who stay in holiday lets are very loyal to the owners and may well include a significant number of friends and acquaintances. There is a possibility that you will lose some of this business initially; building up your own band of regular visitors may well take several years.

Buying a business with potential for growth

The potential to increase turnover may come from several areas:

Increasing bookings
Improve peak season occupancy through:

● better, targeted advertising;

● increasing the level of advertising spend;

● investing in new brochures and other promotional material.

Extending the season
Factors to bear in mind are:

● additional wear and tear on your units, especially over the wet winter months.

- additional heating costs.

- are the units suitable for out-of-season lettings?

- how will you attract out-of-season guests? What can you offer – wet weather facilities (games room, indoor pool), drying room (for walkers), proximity to towns, etc.?

- will you need to incur additional marketing costs to reach what is effectively a different sector of the market?

If you do try to extend the season, don't forget to allow yourself time during the off-season for essential maintenance and decorating.

The tariffs you can charge in the off-season period are going to be much lower than the high season rates. A cottage that lets for, say, £400 per week during the summer may make £125–£150 during the winter. You have to analyse whether the additional income is worth the additional cost plus the additional work involved in staying open.

It is probably worth noting that out-of-season visitors can be very loyal and generate a lot of repeat, albeit low value, business. During the autumn, for example, you may find that your guests are mainly couples looking for a quiet break. They may well have already had a summer holiday, going to a different destination each year. But for their off-season break they want to go to a place where they know the accommodation and know the people, and where they know that they will be comfortable. These visitors tend to come back year after year.

Upgrading the accommodation
Additional income can be earned by upgrading the standard of accommodation and hence charging a higher tariff or attracting a larger number of guests.

Before you embark on any upgrades, consider:

- the costs of upgrading vs the benefits;

- the impact on existing repeat customers – will they be happy to pay extra or will you potentially lose some business?

- if you are upgrading to a higher quality level, your advertising, marketing and everything else about your business must be in step with this new image.

Upgrading other facilities
The equation is always whether the expenditure incurred justifies the work. Each situation will have to be judged on its own merits. Some additional facilities may extend the season, enable a higher tariff to be charged, or just give you a competitive edge when it comes to a potential customer choosing your accommodation.

Adding accommodation
Are there existing buildings or units that can be converted to provide extra accommodation? This will generate additional income immediately and will have the biggest impact on turnover, but consider:

● upfront costs vs benefits over a number of years;

● impact on existing accommodation while work is being carried out;

● impact on the site as a whole;

● do you think you can fill the additional accommodation – is there a market?

If you do decide to expand in this way, try to avoid mixing different quality accommodation; for example, don't be tempted to put in some budget family units where you already have top-end accommodation. This may initially sound like a good idea, effectively diversifying into different markets, but in practice this gives out very mixed messages in terms of how you market your accommodation, and potentially gives you problems in managing your site.

Diversifying the business
Another way of generating additional income is to look at other potential sources of revenue from the property. Examples include:

● bed and breakfast;

● tea rooms;

● meal service, restaurant or bar;

● running short residential courses;

● opening a gallery, craft shop or exhibition space.

CASE STUDY

Fiona and Michael almost get diverted

There is chalet park among the first set of agents' particulars that Fiona and Michael receive. The site is in an excellent location and comprises the chalets, an owners' house, several outbuildings and five acres of amenity land. Fiona and Michael view the property: they fall in love with the house and are excited by the prospect of converting one of the outbuildings into a small leisure complex, for which planning permission already exists.

However, they do some research and discover that the cost of converting the outbuildings to a leisure complex is much higher than they first imagined. When they analyse the situation, they realise that the leisure complex will not bring in any significant extra income. The chalets tend to be fully booked during the summer holidays, and they are not suitable for use during the winter months. Also, the chalets tend to cater for value-for-money, family holidays so there is little scope to increase tariffs following the addition of the leisure suite.

A chalet site never really coincided with the type of business they wanted to run, and they realise that they had been carried away by the potential of the site and the house. Reluctantly, they decide that this property is not for them and they decide only to view those properties that meet their original specification for high quality cottages.

MAKING A DECISION

When it comes to making a decision about a property, the most important thing is to take your time. Don't be rushed into buying something that isn't right – it's easy to panic when you start to despair of ever finding the right place.

For a self-catering complex, it is not uncommon for people to look for one or two years, or even longer, before they find the right property. At any one time, there aren't a vast number of self-catering properties on the market, and as this is going to be both your life and your livelihood, you have to get it right, even if it takes longer than you think. It is also worth bearing in mind that it may not be so easy to sell up if you have made a mistake – again, it could take several years to find the right buyer.

Making a decision will involve consideration of:

● whether it is the right place to live;

- whether it is the right place for the whole family;

- whether it is the right business proposition.

Inevitably, you will have to do some financial modelling, refining your figures as you go along. One of your prime considerations will be whether the business will provide sufficient profit for your needs and for the level of investment you are thinking of making.

But, however logical you try to be, you can't ignore your instincts. You may well come across a property that you fall in love with. But try to be logical, and keep asking yourself the same fundamental questions. Is this the sort of business I want to run? Can we make this work from a business point of view?

Be brutal. Rule out the non-starters, the properties that won't earn you a living and the properties that you have doubts about, and don't waste valuable time on them.

Making comparisons

If you have several properties under consideration, there are several ways of gathering your thoughts together. It may be useful for you to draw up a comparison table (see Figure 4).

There are many other techniques which help in decision-making, and some are listed below. These may seem simplistic, but you may well find that at the very least a systematic look at your choices may provoke discussion and analysis of what you are attracted to – and why.

	Value of house £000	Value of units £000	Total selling price £000	Number of letting units	Annual income £000	Income per unit £000	Price per unit (excl. house) £000
Sunny Cottages	75	150	225	2	12	6	75
Mill Holidays	No house	300	300	10	45	4.5	30
Valley Chalets	125	250	375	20	60	3	12.5

Fig. 4. Comparing properties.

Listing out the pros and cons
Make a simple list on a piece of paper divided down the middle with pros and cons on either side. Do the positives outweigh the negatives? Are any of the negatives so major as to rule out the property altogether?

Allocating a score
This can be useful if there is more than one person involved in the decision-making. Decide on some basic criteria, for example location, schools, opportunities to expand, business viability. Each person assigns a mark out of five for each item and the resulting scores can then be compared.

Using a SWOT analysis
A technique often used in marketing, this is an analysis of strengths, weaknesses, opportunities and threats (see Figure 5). It looks at the current position (strengths and weaknesses) and the future – what opportunities and threats will impact on the future health of the business.

Whatever technique you use to help reach a decision, you will learn a lot from the process itself. Analysing the reasons why you've rejected a property will help you formulate what you do want.

RENOVATING A PROPERTY

Maybe you already own a derelict building that's ripe for conversion, or perhaps you are looking to buy a property to renovate. This is an exciting thing to do, but also a very stressful experience for a lot of people. It can be very easy to underestimate the time, the energy and the money

Strengths	**Weaknesses**
10 mins from beach	Too close to main road?
Large units – family sized	Units need upgrading – cost?
Opportunities	**Threats**
Also do B&B – good location for passing trade?	Decline of traditional seaside holidays in this area?
Upgrade and do out of season specials?	Area already well-provided with self-catering

Fig. 5. Using a SWOT analysis.

that gets swallowed up by a project like this. The great advantage is that, hopefully, you will get something that matches exactly your requirements, designed the way you want it.

Preparing to renovate a property

Before you start, try to talk to people who have been in this situation and ask them for their advice. There are also specialist magazines that deal with self-build and conversions which provide a good source of ideas and product information.

Look at other properties for ideas. Be very specific about the uses of the building. Inevitably, there will be a trade-off between what you want and what you can afford. The more specific you can be, the easier the work of your architect and builder and the more likely you are to get the finished building that you want. If the property is going to be used solely for holiday lets, then the specification may be different from a property that you are converting with a view, for example, to letting before you live in it as your family home.

But with holiday lets, it's inevitably the more mundane issues – practicality, ease of maintenance and cleaning – that tend to come high up the list of requirements.

CASE STUDY

George decides on two units

After initial discussions with an architect, George has to decide whether to convert his main barn into one large unit sleeping six people, or into two smaller units sleeping two and four. At first, he thinks that one larger unit will be better as he won't have to double up on bathrooms, kitchens and living space. But he changes his mind when he talks to other farmers with holiday lets. Because he lives some way from the sea and facilities and tourist attractions in the immediate area are limited, he believes that most of his guests will be couples looking to enjoy the countryside and so smaller units would be better. He also realises that although the individual tariffs will be cheaper, his total letting income each week will be greater by letting out two units instead of one. He talks to his architect and asks him to see whether a connecting door between two smaller units could be incorporated, thus giving the flexibility to join the two units together if required for larger groups.

Getting advice

You will need to get advice, and later on quotes, from a number of builders, plumbers, electricians, architects and so on. If you are already living in the area, you may already have contacts. If not, then start your research early – you will need to start finding people to work with while you are still looking for a property.

Before you finally buy a property, ask an architect or builder to come with you. Discuss your plans and take their advice at this stage as to the feasibility of what you want to do.

When you are evaluating contractors, consider the following:

Costs
Estimates of costs may vary widely. But the cheapest quote may not be the best value or give you the appropriate quality of work. Make sure you understand what is and is not included in the estimate. Don't forget to allow for VAT.

Commitment
Is your job going to be one of many, fitted in around other work? How committed will your contractor be to meeting your deadlines?

Personal relationship
Relationships between builders, architects, contractors and clients can go very sour. Try to make sure right from the outset that communications are good and that you feel comfortable with the people that you're working with and confident in their abilities.

Personal recommendations
Try to use people who are recommended to you. Always ask to see completed work and talk to previous clients. You can also check with the relevant professional or trade association whether the person you are working with has the appropriate registrations and insurance.

Carrying out work yourself
How much work are you going to carry out yourself? Costs can be saved, but you will have to fit in as part of the team involved in the

whole process and you will have to be realistic as to whether you have the appropriate skills to do the job in a professional way.

Meeting deadlines

Realism is the key to a successful conversion. This means realistic cost estimates from your suppliers and builders, and realistic time estimates. If you miss opening at the beginning of a season, this may have a severe impact on your finances. Most of your income for the year will be generated over the space of a few weeks in the summer, and income in your first year will be critical, as this is the time when your expenditure is highest.

Minimising the risks

Be realistic

As well as realistic time and cost estimates, ask your contractors for a worst-case scenario – at least that way you know what the worst could be.

Build in contingencies

Add both time and money contingencies. The extent of building works will never be fully known until work starts and potential problems are uncovered. Make sure your contingencies are sufficient to enable you to fund additional costs and absorb extra time.

Think about your opening date

You will probably be planning to open at the beginning of the season, Easter or sometime soon after. This will give you time to get into a routine before the height of the season. If something goes wrong and you can't open on time, will you be able to find alternative accommodation for your guests nearby?

Think about your costs

Don't underestimate the time and costs of finishing off, furnishing and equipping your units.

Build in testing time

Build time into the plan for test driving your conversion. Either ask friends to test it out or, better still, stay in the unit yourself to make sure everything works as it should.

Keep on top of the job

Make sure you understand how the conversions are progressing, and if things start to go adrift, act immediately.

CASE STUDY

Sue makes a mistake

Sue decides to go ahead with the work needed on her granny flat. Since realising that there is a glut of holiday accommodation in town, she has done more research and now believes that she there is a market for top quality, well-maintained accommodation that can be used for holiday lets and also by local businesses who want to place people in self-catering accommodation in preference to a hotel.

Someone she knows who does some building work looks at the flat and offers to do the job at what seems to be a very reasonable price. The work gets off to a good start, but soon problems start. Work stops while the builder does another job, and Sue is not satisfied with some of the work that has been completed. When she finally pins him down, the builder reacts by saying that he was doing this as a favour and that she can't expect him to stop work on all his other jobs. Work stops. He bills her for the work already done, but it is more than Sue thinks it should be. However, she has no itemised estimate to check with and there was no agreement as to when the money should be paid. Sue starts to search for a new builder, having lost valuable time and money.

ORGANISING FINANCE

This can be a chicken and egg subject – you can't organise any borrowing until you have a specific property in mind and you can't seriously view a property until you know how much and under what conditions you can borrow.

However, you should be able to do a lot of preliminary work in advance and be able to get a good idea of what sort of borrowing, if any, you will need. The most important thing is not to over-extend yourself. Don't borrow at any price. There are many, many self-catering businesses that have failed due to poor cash flow and an inability to make debt repayments. Typical returns on capital are not sufficient to sustain high levels of borrowing.

Advance preparations

Discuss your plans in advance
Discuss your plans in general terms with banks, mortgage brokers and building societies. You would normally start by talking to any institutions with which you already have a relationship, although this is not where you may end up. Get some rough ideas of what they will lend you and what this will cost – this is key information for your financial models as interest payments could well be a large slice of your monthly outgoings.

You will need to go in with some estimated figures for what you are hoping to borrow and what sort of return your business will be expected to achieve. The situation will be very different if you are applying for:

● a mortgage on a house with a small granny flat; or

● a self-catering cottage complex – in which case, you may well be looking at a commercial loan and the preparation of a robust business case.

Do your research
One of the first things you need to research are interest rates for the particular kind of financing you are looking for.

There are many different financial products on the market and new products are being developed all the time. By all means look at all the options available to you, but don't get involved in sophisticated financial products unless you have a very clear understanding of the mechanics and the potential downsides of any particular arrangement.

Be prepared
Go into any meetings with potential lenders as well prepared as possible. Inevitably, at an early stage, most of your numbers will be based on assumptions. Don't be afraid of making assumptions, but make sure they're realistic, be clear about the assumptions you've made, and if necessary present scenarios of what may happen under buoyant and under poor trading conditions. For further information see Chapter 4: Preparing a Business Plan.

CHECKLIST

● Before you start looking at properties:
  – start defining exactly what you are looking for;

– start getting a feel for the property market in your chosen area.

● When you are looking at properties:
  – prepare a checklist of questions to ask;
  – keep a record of each property you view.

● If you are renovating, start planning the work and contacting professionals and contractors.

● Start thinking about financing your business and how much you may need to borrow.

4

Preparing a Business Plan

If you need to borrow money from a lender, then you will almost certainly need to draft a business plan. Even if you don't need a business plan for the bank, think about preparing one anyway:

- It will force you to think clearly about the business you are going into, who your customers are and how you will reach them.

- It will give you the impetus to start researching and formulating the financial figures.

- It will force you to start thinking about the risks and sensitivities inherent in the business.

- It will give you a structure around which to gather your thoughts.

- It will help you formulate your objectives.

- It will force you into thinking about the medium- and long-term prospects for the business.

Most banks and building societies have booklets, spreadsheets and specimen layouts for business plans and will give advice regarding the preparation of a plan. Obviously, it makes sense to use the format favoured by a particular lender. For this reason, this chapter concentrates on the contents of your business plan rather than prescribing a particular layout.

Whatever layout you use, some elements will be common. You will need:

- a description of your business and your business objectives;

- an analysis of your target markets and how you will reach them;

- a set of financial forecasts, both short and longer term.

DRAFTING A MARKETING PLAN

This essentially is an analysis of the service you are offering, who your customers are and how you intend to reach them.

Describing your business

You will need to cover:

- the type of holiday business you're in;
- the location and general description of the property;
- what level of service and quality you will be offering – and at what price.

Defining your business objectives

Examples could include:

- to provide high quality accommodation that offers excellent value for money to customers;

- to move into profit during the second year of trading;

- to target return bookings at 30 per cent for year 2, 40 per cent for year 3 and 50 per cent by year 5.

Identifying your target customers

It is essential that you know who your customers are.

- Age, family situation, their holiday requirements.

- Are you targeting any particular sector of the market – and what are the prospects for this sector?

Reaching your target customers

This will need to outline:

- your marketing and advertising strategy.

CASE STUDY

Fiona and Michael find a property

Fiona and Michael believe that they have found a property to buy. Their bank has already agreed in principle to a commercial loan; they now need to prepare a business plan. They start working on the marketing section; their first draft follows.

Draft marketing plan for Cartwheel Cottages

The business
Cartwheel Cottages is a complex of converted farm buildings located in a courtyard setting with five acres of adjoining land. There are six letting units, sleeping between two and six people. The business currently trades May to October only, and achieves an average of 16 weeks bookings per cottage.

Advertising spend is low and little has been invested in the units for the last five years or so. There is little repeat business.

The plan
The surveyor's report is generally favourable and the courtyard is potentially very attractive. There is scope to update and modernise the cottages, and greatly increase the level of business.

Key elements of the plan are:

1 To refurbish the cottages to a very high standard, using country fabrics, antiques, four-poster beds and so on to create a classic, comfortable English look.

2 To apply for English Tourism Council quality grading, planning the refurbishment to aim for the highest possible classification.

3 To landscape approximately one acre of the land to provide a fine garden setting.

4 To manage the cottages ourselves (it is currently managed on an arm's length basis) to ensure that guests receive the highest standards of care and attention.

5 To open year round, offering short breaks and specialist holidays in the shoulder and off-peak seasons.

The market

We will be targeting mature couples, taking advantage of the ever-increasing 'grey pound', overseas visitors looking for a taste of England's heritage, as well as families in the summer who can take advantage of the wide range of activities in the area.

Although there is a lot of holiday accommodation in the area, we believe that we have:

- an ideal location, perfect for touring the region's attractions, and easy access to the antique shops, the stately homes and gardens which will appeal to our target customers;

- a good proposition for a sound, year-round business;

- a plan to upgrade the cottages that will put them at the top end of the holiday let sector: our research shows that there is actually very little accommodation of this type in the area;

- scope for future expansion into guided excursions to homes and gardens, gardening and antiques courses, providing a top quality meal service and specialising in providing honeymoon and anniversary romantic breaks.

Our advertising

We plan to:

- have professionally designed, high quality brochures to advertise our accommodation;

- take regular advertising space in appropriate quality, national magazines;

- make use of the Internet to advertise the cottages, linking through to the region's attractions and providing information on things to do, places to visit, restaurants and so on. This is the main route by which we plan to reach our overseas customers;

- aim for a high level of repeat business and referrals: 40 per cent after two years.

Exercise

Read through this draft plan critically.

1. Is there anything more you'd like to know about the business?

2. Fiona and Michael realise that this draft contains no actual statistics or figures to back up their case. They decide to refer to appendices: what kind of figures should they include?

3. Do you think that Fiona and Michael have thought through their advertising plan in sufficient detail? Are there any weaknesses in their proposal? What other advertising strategies might they consider?

UNDERSTANDING PROFIT AND CASH FLOW

If you have no experience in finance, putting together a financial plan can appear very daunting. If you don't feel confident in this area, there are many sources of help, from accountants, enterprise agencies, Business Links and banks as well as numerous books and courses.

There are three main financial forecasts that you will need to prepare:

- a profit and loss account;

- a balance sheet; and

- a cash flow forecast.

The profit and loss account shows how much profit you plan to make over a given period. It shows what you have left after deducting expenses associated with running your business and after deducting 'non-cash' items such as depreciation.

The balance sheet is a snapshot taken at the end of a period of your assets and liabilities and the funding of your business.

But in a small start-up business, the most important thing is having the cash to pay the bills. Keeping a positive cash flow will be one of your main targets during the initial phases of your business.

It is perfectly possible for a business making a profit on paper to suffer cash flow problems. An example may help to clarify this.

During the year, Stream Cottages has a projected turnover of £15,000. The forecast profit the first year is is shown in Figure 6.

On the face of things, a small profit has been made. This could be interpreted as a reasonably successful first year.

But this was the first year's trading for the business. The property was purchased in October, but there was no advertising in place, and hence no booking income, until the New Year. Cash flow – the actual payments

Stream Cottages: Forecast profit and loss account		
	£	£
Income		15,000
Expenditure		
Staff costs	3,000	
Business rates	3,000	
Advertising	2,000	
Electricity	1,000	
Maintenance	2,000	
Sundries	1,000	
Depreciation	500	
Total expenditure	12,500	12,500
Profit before tax and drawings	2,500	

Fig. 6.   A forecast profit statement.

in and out – for the first three months looked like Figure 7.

With initial capital of £3,000, this business would be in severe financial trouble before the end of the second month of trading – a very serious position, probably requiring negotiation of an overdraft with the bank, with extra finance charges to pay which would in turn eat into the small projected profit for the year.

Cash flow, then, is primarily a matter of timing – when is money due to come in and when will it be going out. In this example, all the expenditure is 'front-loaded' – i.e. it isn't spread evenly through the year but falls substantially in the early part of trading. This is a common pattern with new businesses where early trading sees high levels of expenditure and low income.

The question is whether you can fund those periods of time when cash flow is negative, i.e. expenditure is greater than income. This will be a key area in your plan.

FORECASTING INCOME AND EXPENDITURE

At the outset, you will not know for certain what your income and expenditure will be. But you have to make some guesses; forecasting is all about making reasonable assumptions and updating your forecasts as more information becomes available.

Stream Cottages: Cash flow statement

	Oct £	Nov £	Dec £
Income	Nil	Nil	Nil
Expenditure			
Rates	300	300	300
Advertising	1,000		
Staff costs	250	250	250
Maintenance	400	400	400
Electricity	75	75	75
Net cash outflow	2,025	1,025	1,025
Opening bank balance	3,000	975	(50)
Closing bank balance	975	(50)	(1,075)

Fig. 7. A cash flow statement.

Turnover

Part of your research will involve understanding the economics of your type of business. The most important thing to do in terms of forecasting is to compare yourself to like businesses – there is little point in comparing tariffs and occupancy rates between a beach front cottage with indoor pool and sauna and a log cabin in the country, even if they are just a few miles apart. Key components of your income forecast are as follows.

Tariffs
What will you be able to charge for high, medium and low season? Look at what similar businesses are charging. If you are buying an existing business, what are their charges? Are there any additional charges – for pets, video hire or whatever – and are these significant enough to include in your forecast? Will you be offering discounts for repeat business, long stays or late bookings, for example, and will these have a significant impact on turnover? Will your tariff include electricity and gas or will separate payment be made?

Occupancy
The best way of looking at this is probably in terms of number of weeks,

although percentage occupancies are sometimes used. Typical occupancies will vary hugely around the country, and even within a very small geographical area, between, for example, a rural and a coastal site. You need to understand what is typical for your type of business in your location. As a guideline, a small, single cottage with limited marketing may well let for 16 weeks per annum, while a coastal complex with all-weather facilities may let 40 weeks per year per unit. Also bear in mind that it will take several years to build towards your target level of occupancy.

Initially, you may need to sign up with an agency. This is often the only way to start out due to problems with the timing of advertising etc., and it may even be a lender's condition for the first few years. An agency will probably be able to give you a good idea of what you should expect to achieve in terms of weeks booked, but double-check the figures they quote you for reasonableness.

A good way to start forecasting is to break your year down and to take a view of the best, worst and most likely trading situations, as in Figure 8.

To translate this occupancy forecast into money terms, the appropriate tariff will need to be applied.

Start-up costs

This will be your front-end expenditure – what it will cost to get yourself in business. Initially, this will be the purchase of land and buildings, fees associated with buying the business (legal fees, search fees, surveys, land registry, stamp duty), the costs of internal and external renovations and repairs, and initial equipment and fixtures.

Recurring costs

These are the normal running costs of the business, some of which will fall annually, e.g. charges for annual guide books and membership fees for trade associations, and some quarterly or monthly, e.g. utility bills. Some of these are fixed costs that you will have to pay regardless of whether you have any guests or not, for example insurance and business rates. Others are variable costs – they vary with occupancy, for example electricity usage.

To get an idea of forecast expenditure, again, owners of the same sort of business, previous owners of an existing business and your own experience will be the best guides. Taxation units of local councils will give

Occupancy forecast – Y1 trading			
	No. of weeks booked		
Assumptions	*Best case*	*Worst case*	*Most likely case*
Assume fully booked during summer holidays	7	7	7
For Christmas/Easter/Half term weeks	8	4	5
For shoulder weeks – June and September	8	2	4
Low season breaks	10	3	6
Total forecast weeks booked	33	16	22

Fig. 8. Using scenarios to forecast occupancy.

a view on business rates and utility companies may help with information about usage and tariffs. Don't forget to include amounts in your forecasts for ongoing replacement of furniture, fixtures and fittings, etc.

Do as much research as you can. Make assumptions and base forecasts on those numbers. As you progress you will start to get a better idea of actual costs and you will be able to update the assumptions on which your forecasts are based.

Some ongoing cost items to consider are:

● advertising

● postage

● stationery and printing

● repairs

● maintenance

● decorating

● telephone, electricity, gas, water charges

- business rates

- gardening and landscaping

- staff costs

- insurance – contents, buildings, public liability, employer's liability

- transport costs

- replacement of furniture, fixtures and fittings

- cleaning materials, specialist cleaning charges

- membership fees, inspection charges

- finance charges and interest payments.

Preparing a cash flow forecast

Timing is crucial here – when are you going to pay your bills? When will you receive your income?

To forecast when you will receive your income, you will need to make some assumptions about when people book and when they will pay for their accommodation. You will also need to decide about your deposit policy: normally, you would be expecting people to pay a deposit, plus a balance some time in advance of their holiday.

For your forecast you will need to make some general assumptions: don't get too complicated at this stage, but just recognise that there will be income coming into the business in advance of the holiday season.

When will most bookings be taken? In general, the period January through to March generates the largest numbers of bookings for the summer and you would expect to receive quite a high proportion of deposit income during this time. Bookings for the spring, autumn and short breaks are generally booked much closer to the time where they are taken and so the timing impact on the cash flow will be less; for forecasting purposes, it will probably be reasonable to assume that income falls in the same month as the holiday is taken.

Preparing a profit and loss forecast

When compiling a profit and loss forecast, the issue of timing is a different one. Expenditure and income are recognised in the accounts in the period to which they relate. A holiday taken in July will generate income in July, regardless of when the actual money is received. The same logic applies on the expenditure side: if an insurance bill, for example, is paid in February Year 1 but the policy runs from April Y2 onwards, the expenditure will be shown in the Y2 profit and loss account, but the Y1 cash flow.

The other main adjustment needed in a profit and loss statement is for non-cash items, principally depreciation. If an asset used in the business, e.g. a van, is purchased for cash, the cash flow will show the entire amount as expenditure in the month that the cash is paid out. However, the business will benefit from that van for a number of years, and so the cost of the van in the profit and loss account will be spread over those years. There are several ways of calculating depreciation. One simple method is to divide the cost of the asset equally between the number of years it will be used in the business.

Reviewing your forecasts

Having prepared all your forecasts, it is now a case of making sure that the business will generate enough money for you to live on. This will require a serious look at your own personal expenditure. Don't forget that out of the profits of the business you will have to:

- reinvest in the business: continual upgrades are required;

- replace assets: car, laundry equipment and so on;

- pay yourself a wage: termed 'drawings' if you are operating as a sole trader or partnership;

- pay your tax bill;

- pay your self-employed National Insurance contributions;

- make provision for a pension and possibly private medical cover.

ASSESSING THE RISKS

You should consider the risks of a new venture. What happens if your forecast of bookings turns out to be wildly optimistic? What if your expenditure forecast is too low?

Sensitivities

You need to consider the extent to which a change in one item of your forecast will impact on overall profitability. For example, you may find that your water bill forecast is low by 50 per cent. This sounds quite a lot, but in reality it might be that your actual bill is £300 against a forecast of £200. Profits will be £100 lower than you thought, but how significant is this? On the other hand, if booking income is 50 per cent lower than anticipated, this will have a huge impact on your forecast profitability.

The important thing is to spend time and effort analysing the most sensitive areas of your plan. Work out how much these items will have to change to make a significant impact. Spend time on getting the forecast for these critical factors correct.

PUTTING IT ALL TOGETHER

Inevitably, you will have a lot of information by the time you have gathered all your research and your projections together.

Your final business plan has to strike the right balance between giving enough information and giving too much. Probably the best approach to take is to spend time preparing a good summary; this can be used to highlight key features of your plan. Detailed figures and analyses can then be given as supporting documents.

If you are looking to borrow money, then the summary must be good – you should extract the key points, present a professional image and persuade the lender that you have a reasonable business proposition for him. Only then will he want to look at your supporting detail and analyses. Make sure that everything is well presented and that the lender doesn't have to work hard to understand the numbers.

The ultimate success of most small businesses is largely in the hands of one individual – you, the owner. Any potential lender is going to look for the personal attributes, the skills and the experience you have that will make the business succeed. Your business plan is one of the most important ways that you can impress him with your professionalism.

If you are borrowing money, your business plan should:

● Be realistic but conservative. You don't want to seem over-optimistic. On the other hand, if your plan is too pessimistic, you may have problems persuading your lender that you have a viable proposition.

● Give you sufficient funds. Make sure that you are borrowing enough money to cover your needs – if you're asking for cash to fund start-up costs, are you also going to have enough to fund working capital requirements during the start-up phase? No lender is going to be impressed if you go back for more cash within a matter of months.

We have talked a lot in this chapter about using the business plan for lending. Don't forget that your plan is a valuable tool for you to actively use in the management of your business.

CASE STUDY

Sue prepares a plan

Due to the additional costs that Sue has incurred in building works, she realises that she will have to ask for a bank loan of £1,000 in order to complete the work. She decides that she will prepare a business plan to present to her bank manager.

Her first draft runs to 30 pages. She realises that given the relatively small amount she wants to borrow, this is far too long. She revises her plan, and ends up with four main pages, plus supporting schedules to back up her numbers if she needs them.

Although her first draft was too long, she realises that the work she put into producing it was extremely valuable. As a result of her analysis, she is satisfied that her forecast and assumptions are sound, and as a result she feels more confident about the venture she is undertaking.

She uses this work as the basis for an internal plan, a document that she will use to keep track of her business.

CHECKLIST

● Decide on a format for your business plan, looking at recommended layouts supplied by your bank as a first step.

● Prepare your financial forecasts.

● Draft your plan and review it for completeness and accuracy.

● Use the plan on an ongoing basis to help you manage your business.

5

Getting Ready for Business

SETTING PRIORITIES

You have a property in mind and the finance in place to make a start. The temptation is to jump straight in, but some time spent setting your priorities at the outset will save you headaches later. Whatever work you are carrying out, there are two golden rules:

- the work will expand to fit the time available (and more); and

- everything will take much longer than you think, especially if you are doing a lot of work yourself.

When you prioritise your work, think about dividing it into work you must do, for example providing the appropriate standards of accommodation and dealing with safety issues, and work that it would be nice to do in an ideal world. Don't spend time on the 'nice to do' items until the essentials are taken care of.

Planning your marketing

However much building or renovation work you have to do, don't forget the lead times for advertising and brochures. A perfectly restored or decorated property is going to be of little use if no one knows about it. There are long lead times for advertisements; for example, for some annual publications, the deadline may be as early as June the previous year.

Bear in mind the following when you are planning your advertising:

- Ideally, some of your advertising needs to be in place immediately after Christmas, traditionally the time when people start thinking about summer holidays. If you can't achieve this, don't despair –

there are always people who leave booking their holidays to the last minute.

- You need to have brochures, booking forms and tariff sheets ready for when people start to respond to your adverts.

CASE STUDY

Fiona and Michael plan their brochures

Fiona and Michael face a dilemma. The interior decoration and furnishings of their cottages will be a major selling point and they want to feature interior photographs in their brochure. They are advertising from January onwards and need to have a brochure ready for then, but the upgrades are not finished and so they aren't in a position to take interior photographs; in any case, they would prefer to wait until the weather improves before they take their exterior photographs.

They decide as a stopgap measure to produce a temporary brochure themselves, set up on their PC and printed on a good quality colour printer. The initial brochures will feature exterior shots and pictures of the area, which they hope to source from the local tourist board.

As soon as possible, they plan to stage some interior photos: even if work isn't finished, they think they will be able to put something together to give people a feel for their cottages. They are already working with a designer on a draft brochure layout and copy so that they can go ahead with the full colour brochure as soon as they get their photographs done.

Although they realise that this isn't an ideal solution, they don't want to spend a lot of money on professionally produced brochures until the cottages are exactly as they want them. They hope that this will not impact too much on their first season's bookings, but feel that this is their only real option.

The plan is to have their full brochure ready for the summer, for this year's guests to take away with them.

Planning your other work

If you are carrying out conversions or renovation work, you will have a programme of work tied into the various elements of the build. When looking at your overall schedules, don't forget that the finishing off work can take far longer than you think. Some things you need to think about in advance include the following:

- Lead times for planning permission etc.

- Services – building contractors, plumbers, electricians and so on. Try to select your contractors in advance and find out whether they will be able to start work when you need them. If you are moving from the city into the country, don't necessarily bank on work being carried out at city levels of urgency.

- Building materials – will anything need to be specially ordered?

- Furniture – is there somewhere that you can source furniture from stock? Again, if you have particular requirements for items that need to be ordered, don't forget to put these into your plan.

- Staff – you will need to get your staffing organised well in advance, even if you only need a cleaner for a few hours a week. In some tourist areas, there is a real shortage of reliable, seasonal staff, from cleaners through to chefs, and this is compounded if you live in a rural area where people need to own a car to get to you. You may need to organise a pick-up service if this is the case. If you advertise for staff early, you have more chance of getting good, reliable people, even if it means taking them on earlier than you really need them, or perhaps paying a retainer.

For each unit, look at the work that needs to be done, the order it needs to be done in, and try to realistically estimate how long the work is going to take. You can map this out on a chart, looking at key dates and key events (see Figure 9). This doesn't have to be anything sophisticated, but unless you do this you will never know whether your overall deadlines are realistic or not.

CASE STUDY

Sue's opening date is under threat

Sue's new builder starts work in her flat, but after a week, he rings to say that he has to finish another job and won't be able to be with her for a while. Sue looks at her plan. The building work will still be done in time, but she will have less time to decorate, which she was going to do herself in order to save some money. When she looks at her diary, she realises that the time she now has for decorating falls when other staff at the hospital are on holiday and so she will have to cover more shifts. She

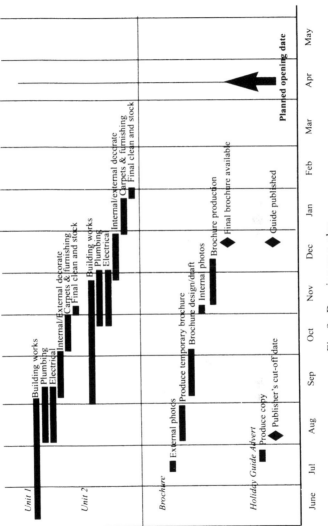

Fig. 9. Drawing up a plan.

realises that it will be very difficult to finish the decorating herself.

She considers her options. She can find another builder who can start immediately, but she doesn't feel she has time to do this. She can delay her opening date, losing income as a result, or she can employ someone to do the decorating instead of her, again at more expense than planned. She decides on this last option, and also to delay opening by a week to give her some contingency. She calls her builder and presses him for a guarantee on when he will complete the remaining work, and starts to look for a decorator who will commit to working as soon as the building work is complete.

Even with the extra week she has built in, Sue still feels that there is a risk to her opening date and decides to keep everything under close review. She draws up a new plan and from that she makes a list of jobs for the coming week. At the end of each week, she reviews her lists and plans for the week ahead.

TAKING OVER AN EXISTING BUSINESS

If you are buying an existing business, your plans will need to address the following.

What immediate work needs doing?

Do the properties meet safety and legal requirements? Do you need to upgrade/add facilities/redecorate? Don't forget that existing bookings will have been made on the existing level and quality of facilities, in which case it might be best to trade for a season without making any changes and upgrade during the following winter.

When do you plan to do the work?

Bear in mind that once the season starts you will only have access to a unit on changeover day when there is very little time available to do anything except quick repairs. Also, if you have more than one flat or cottage located together, you will not want to work on one while the other is occupied; people don't want to come on holiday to find the builders in next door. At best, your work will be limited to the times when other guests are out.

If you decide to keep the property in its current state until the following season, take the opportunity to ask your guests what things they would like to see changed, perhaps in a questionnaire, and very importantly, whether they would be prepared to pay extra to have extra facilities. Moving upmarket may well lose you good customers from the past.

What are the arrangements for taking over existing bookings?

It is highly likely if you are taking over an existing business that it will come with some bookings already made. In this case, it is normal practice for deposits and final payments applicable to the period after you take over to be transferred to you from the current owner.

It is good practice to write to those clients who have already booked informing them of the change of ownership. This may well be best as a joint letter from you and the previous owner, and is essential where a final payment is due and you need to change the name of the person or establishment to whom cheques are made out. Also consider a letter to regular customers, introducing yourself and assuring them that previous standards will be maintained.

Ideally, you will need to spend time with the previous owner. Amongst the many items you should consider are:

- bookings in hand: contact details, dates booked, amounts paid and payable, special requirements;

- any stock items to be carried over;

- an inventory of fixtures and fittings included in the sale;

- details of previous guests and regular clients;

- details of any agency agreements in place;

- details of recommended builders, tradesmen and suppliers;

- details of current staff;

- details of the workings of the units: electricity, waste disposal, fuse boxes, manholes, plumbing, etc. – ideally with plans;

- details of the routine involved in running the establishment;

● guarantees and warranties, operating instructions and any other paperwork that has future value to the business.

Also, make arrangements for the owner to agree to leave stocks of brochures, forms and so on. You may well want to print your own, but this will take time and a stock of stationery will see you through your early days.

When you take over a business, you will have lots of ideas about what you want to change. Don't rush into things. Take time to see how things work and to sort out priorities.

PREPARING YOUR PROPERTY

When you start to think about preparing your property you should be aware of all the relevant legislation that may impact on your business – see Chapter 8, 'Asking the Experts'.

If you are starting from scratch and you have more than one unit, take the opportunity to standardise all your kitchen equipment, furnishings, linen and so on from the outset – it makes life simpler and greatly reduces the number of spare items you need to keep.

Where you source your items is a matter of personal preference and to some extent will depend on what is available to you locally. Some things to consider are:

Durability

Items must be able to withstand heavy use. Look carefully at buttons and knobs: how robust are they?

Easy cleaning

Consider washable loose covers for furnishings, washable blankets, easy-clean ovens and hobs, washable lampshades and so on.

Simplicity

Ensure that your appliances are as simple and straightforward as possible. This means less to go wrong and less room for operator error – don't forget that people will probably be unfamiliar with your particular types of appliances.

Instructions

You should provide clear operating instructions for all appliances and other equipment. If you're using a leaflet that came with the product, make sure that you keep a photocopy to replace the original if it gets lost or spoiled.

Buying second-hand

Be aware that if you are buying second-hand, all furnishings and electrical goods must comply with the relevant legislation.

Keeping records

Make a note of what you buy, date and place of purchase, and any guarantees or warranties in place.

What to buy

Inventories from letting agents and requirements for English Tourism Council quality standards can be a useful guide to how you should stock your units. Don't be tempted to over-furnish your units: not every space has to be filled, people have food, belongings and so on to find a place for. And if you put in lots of equipment, remember that these items also have to be checked each week and maintained.

As well as the obvious items, consider the following:

● laundry facilities – Somewhere to wash, dry and iron clothes is very important, especially for families with children;

● providing cleaning materials, buckets, vacuum cleaners, brooms – these items give guests the opportunity to clear up after themselves.

DECIDING ON TERMS AND CONDITIONS

Look in the back of any package holiday brochure and you'll find pages of small print regarding terms and conditions. With a holiday let, don't overdo it – you don't want those pages and pages of small print to swamp the rest of your details.

You will need to decide the following:

- Payment terms: amount of deposit, when payable, date that balance becomes due, discounts for early bookings, return bookings, long stays and short breaks.

- Cancellation policy.

- Who is/is not welcome: children, pets, single-sex groups.

- Bed linen, table linen, towels – what you will provide, whether or not you will charge, what you expect people to bring themselves.

- Facilities for children: cots, highchairs, fireguards, stair gates, cot linen, baby baths: what you will provide and whether or not you will charge.

- Whether you will allow additional people to stay in the unit, and if so, do you provide a put-you-up and do you charge for this?

- Smoking policy: opinions are likely to be strong in both directions. It is certainly true that many people specify non-smoking accommodation, but smokers take holidays too.

When you draft your terms and conditions, you will also need statements regarding:

- guests' responsibility for their own belongings and cars;

- arrival and departure times;

- your breakages/damages policy;

- guests' responsibility to leave units in a reasonable condition.

If you're in any doubt, ask a solicitor to look at your terms and conditions. Don't forget that any number of disclaimers will not absolve you of your responsibility to provide a safe holiday environment for your guests.

Some of these items are now covered in further detail.

Payments

It is usual to request a deposit to secure a booking – usually a percentage, e.g. 10 per cent, 25 per cent or 50 per cent in advance, with the balance payable at some specified date before arrival. You will need to decide a method of payment: cheques are simplest but credit cards are convenient, especially for taking late bookings, however they are costly to operate. If you decide to look at credit cards, shop around for the best deal and investigate whether you can get discounts through your local trade association or small business organisation.

How will you get payments from overseas guests? Options include sterling drafts, Eurocheques or direct transfer into your bank; in the latter case, will you or your guest pay the bank charges?

You should be very clear in your brochure and booking forms whether you make extra charges over and above your tariffs, either in advance or at the site, for items such as:

- electricity, gas, storage heating, logs
- linen
- towels
- dogs
- cots, high chairs
- video recorders.

The amount that you can charge for electricity is governed by legislation – see Chapter 8.

Cancellation

It is recommended that you encourage people to take out holiday cancellation insurance. This can be done in several ways:

1. By providing guests with a proposal form to send directly to an insurance company. Many companies provide specific UK self-catering policies, and will pay a small commission to you for insurance that your guests take out. In reality, these policies can seem to be poor value; where it is optional, guests often don't take out insurance.
2. An alternative is to take out a form of corporate policy. You, the owner, pay one premium to cover all your guests. You can either bear the cost of this yourself, and tell your guests that their tariff includes cancellation insurance (be careful with this though – you do not want people making 'risky' bookings, thinking that they can always cancel if they need to) or you can ask guests to pay for this cover – it should

work out cheaper for them than buying an individual policy.

If guests cancel and don't have insurance, they are liable for payment of the full cost of their holiday on the due date, unless you can relet the unit, in which case you should refund their payment, less any amounts reasonably incurred by you in reletting the unit, for example on administration or additional advertising.

Children

There is some market for adults-only holidays, but in general, during the school holidays, children will be staying in your units. Out of the school holidays, you will probably find that many guests are families with pre-school children: they are usually looking for the convenience and flexibility of a 'home from home'.

Providing equipment
Most holiday lets provide cots and high chairs on request. Do you have the space to put in cots? Will you provide cot bedding or (more usually) will you ask people to bring their own? You may also need to provide stair gates and fire guards. This type of equipment must comply with the relevant standards.

Safety
How safe are your units and the grounds for children? If there are any potential problems these should be made clear in advance of booking. On arrival, parents should be informed of any potential hazards in the units or in the grounds, for example a pond.

Swimming pools are an area of considerable concern – see Chapter 8. Also consider access to your site. Do warning notices need to be posted to warn drivers of children playing nearby?

As an additional safety measure, you may also consider providing plastic beakers and plates in the units, especially where there is an outside patio.

Providing a play area for children
Indoor facilities are always appreciated for days when the weather is bad. Any outdoor play equipment must be safe to use and must be inspected regularly.

Dogs

Whether you accept dogs or not is essentially a matter of personal choice. Many people like to bring their dogs on holiday and this can be a good source of business. To some extent, whether you take dogs or not will depend on the location and type of business you're running. For example, a rural location in good walking country may be very attractive to dog-owners.

If you do decide to accept dogs, then the enjoyment of other guests must not be compromised. For this reason, it is usual to have specific dog rules, typically:

- that dogs shouldn't be left unattended;

- that they should be kept on leads in public areas;

- that they shouldn't be allowed on furniture or in bedrooms;

- that they should be exercised in a specific area, and any mess cleared up – in which case you may need to give thought to dog litter bins, providing pooper-scoopers, etc.

It is a fact that dogs mean extra cleaning, and you may need to deal with doggie smells, accidents, scratched woodwork and furniture.

You may also need to think about limiting numbers of dogs, both in total and in any individual unit.

Accepting other pets

Sometimes people do ask to bring their cats: this needs careful thought and is not something that most owners would allow, however much they like animals! There are inevitably problems with a cat being left indoors with a litter tray, sleeping on the furniture and so on.

It may be useful to have an arrangement with a local cattery so that you can recommend somewhere that cats can be boarded but where owners can visit their animals.

PLANNING YOUR HOUSEKEEPING

There are various decisions you need to make about housekeeping, particularly how you arrange your changeover day and how you organise linen.

Keeping an inventory

You will need to make an inventory for each room, initially to help you with purchasing and then as an ongoing record of what you have in each unit (see Figure 10).

Kitchen Inventory		
Cutlery	Matching sets One per person plus one spare	Table knife and fork; soup and dessertspoon; teaspoon; carving, bread and general purpose knives; salad servers; serving spoons.
Cooking	Size/number suitable for number of guests	Small, medium, large saucepans; milk pan; frying pans; Pyrex/casserole dishes; roasting/baking tins; pie dish; vegetable dishes.
Utensils		Wooden spoons; masher, ladle, fish slice, tongs; potato peeler; whisk; sieve; colander; corkscrew and bottle opener; grater; tea strainer; lemon squeezer; rolling pin; scissors; garlic press.
Crockery	Matching sets One per person plus one spare	Cup and saucer, mug, dinner plate, side plate, cereal bowl, eggcup.
Misc. equipment		Tea pot; tray; butter dish; sugar bowl; milk jug; measuring jug; bread bin; chopping board(s); storage tins/jars; fruit bowl and dishes; condiment set; place mats.
Electrical		Kettle; toaster; microwave; liquidiser; coffee maker; vacuum cleaner; iron & ironing board
Glassware	One set per person plus one spare	Large and small tumblers; beer and wine glasses; jug.
Cleaning		Kitchen bin and bin liners; washing-up bowl and cloths; dustpan and brush; broom; mop; clothes line, clothes airer and pegs; dusters and floor cloths; cleaning fluids.
Linen		Oven glove; tea towels
Miscellaneous		Smoke alarm; fire blanket; fire extinguisher; torch; first aid kit.

Fig. 10.   A sample kitchen inventory.

Deciding on changeover day

You need to decide on a changeover day, normally on a Friday (easier for travelling) or Saturday (more popular as it fits with the normal working week). The day you choose may depend on your other work commitments. Staffing, too, can be an issue. It can be easier to get cleaners to work on a Friday when children are at school than on a Saturday.

If you have a number of units, you may decide to split the changeover day, making it much easier for you to supervise the work. Out of season, you may decide to be flexible about arrival and departure days, according to what guests request, but bear in mind that this can cause disruption to the weeks on either side.

Organising your linen

The linen you provide must be in keeping with the rest of your offering. It is nice for people to arrive to made-up beds, although some operators provide linen for people to make up their own beds, or ask people to provide their own linen, or charge for the hire of linen.

Sheets and blankets vs duvets
It is easier to get a good finish with blankets and bedspreads, but there is more linen overall. Duvets are quicker to deal with on changeover day. If you are using duvets, you will also need to provide blankets for cold weather.

Protecting your beds
Mattress protectors (waterproof on children's beds), pillow protectors and duvet protectors are all well worth the investment. They can be quickly washed if necessary on changeover day and will extend the life of all your bedding items.

Pillows
Invest in good quality pillows and air them regularly. If you have feather pillows, keep some non-allergenic pillows for any guests who have a feather allergy.

Buying linen
Consider how well items will wash, how well they will keep and how easy to iron they are: cheap linen can be a false economy. Fitted sheets will keep down bed making time but will take extra ironing time.

Similarly, ruffled duvet covers and pillowcases may look nice but add to laundering time. You need to consider whether you have adequate washing and drying facilities to do your own laundry; if you have any volume to do, consider investing in a press for the ironing.

When you're costing your linen requirements, bear in mind that you'll need a minimum of two of everything: one set on, the other ready to go on, plus spares.

Using a professional laundry

This may make sense, depending on your volume of linen. Usually, you can either arrange for a pick-up service or you can do your own transportation. This option can be as expensive as hiring linen.

Hiring linen

It is possible to hire linen, towels, tea towels, etc. at around the same cost as having your own linen laundered.

Advantages:

● no work for you

● no start-up purchases

● professional finish – crisp white sheets.

Disadvantages:

● may be a limited range of colours and patterns

● usually there is a minimum weekly charge, so this option wouldn't be suitable for smaller operators.

CASE STUDY

George starts to panic

As George's conversion progresses, he starts to worry about the housekeeping side of the business. He isn't confident that he'll be able to manage this aspect of the business himself and so he advertises in the local village for someone to clean and supervise changeovers. He finds someone suitable, Mrs Owen, and he arranges for her to work all day on Saturdays, starting in advance of his planned opening date, so that she can organise what is needed in terms of linen, cleaning equipment and so on.

Mrs Owen investigates linen hire but the business is not large enough to justify the minimum weekly fee. In the end, she agrees to take on the laundering as well as her other duties; she will come in an extra afternoon during the week to do this. George is happy that this area of the business is now under control, but he realises that he shouldn't rely totally on Mrs Owen in case circumstances change and she is no longer available.

CHECKLIST

● Prioritise your tasks, lay down a plan and review progress regularly.

● If you are taking over an existing business, list the areas where you want a handover from the previous owner. Be very specific.

● Start drafting terms and conditions.

● Start thinking about housekeeping and changeover days

6

Marketing Your Accommodation

Marketing Your Accommodation

Marketing encompasses a range of activities including research, advertising and promotion, public relations, presentation and pricing. The importance of market research has already been covered in Chapter 2. In this chapter, we will primarily be looking at advertising, designing a brochure and the increasing importance of the Internet to small tourism operators.

Probably *the* most important marketing tool you have is yourself. Your personal contact with customers, offering them a warm and friendly, professional service, is a key to your success and may well be the deciding factor between you and a competitor.

Whatever decisions you make in terms of advertising and brochure design, remember the importance of consistency. Make sure that the quality of your advertising matches the quality of the holidays that you're selling and that everything you do fits together as a whole.

SELLING YOUR PRODUCT

You may have the most fabulous holiday cottages available for rent, but unless people know about them, you'll never get the level of business you deserve.

The things you need to consider are as follows:

● How are you going to reach your target market?

● How are you going to persuade them to book with you?

● How are you going to achieve this as cost-effectively as possible?

The trend in the tourism business is away from traditional advertising,

78

such as newspapers and magazines, and towards the Internet. We'll consider traditional methods first: in reality, however committed you are to the new technologies, you probably won't want to abandon this type of advertising all together.

PLANNING YOUR ADVERTISING

Advertising is expensive. You need to spend considerable amounts of money and therefore need to ensure that what you do is effective. To some extent, it is trial and error – what works for some operators won't work for others. But if you keep your target market in mind at all times, you are more likely to come up with a successful advertising strategy.

National newspapers

National newspapers, and particularly the Sundays, run holiday advertising sections. A media pack from the paper will give you an advertising rate card, including details of discounts for series adverts, copy dates and readership profiles from which you can check whether the people who read a given newspaper match the profile of your target guest.

Don't take circulation figures at face value. The number of people who actually read a newspaper is higher than the circulation figure, but not all of these people will actually be looking for a holiday.

Advantages:

● High readership, but not all of these readers will be looking for holidays.

● Can be useful for 'fill-in' weeks – where you have weeks to fill, ads can be placed at short notice.

● Can be cost-effective for larger operators.

Disadvantages:

● Can be expensive. Because of the expense, most small operators use classified ads, with just a few words to sell themselves.

● Short shelf life.

● Can be just one small advertisement amongst many, many others. Best results, however, will come from a regularly placed, small advertisement, rather than a one-off, large display.

If you do take out a classified ad, say as much as you can in very few words. Don't worry about long sentences, go for 'sensory' words, and try to say something a little different from your competitors.

CASE STUDY

Fiona and Michael decide on an advertisement

Although they are anticipating a reasonable first summer, Fiona and Michael are concerned at low levels of off-peak bookings. They decide to run a series of classified advertisements in one of the Sunday papers, specifically targeting autumn breaks and the special weekends they are running. They have 20 words, excluding contact phone number, in which to make their mark. They come up with several drafts:

Draft 1
Log fires, beamed ceilings. Enjoy a relaxing break in our beautiful cottages. Antiques, crafts, cookery weekends. Call for colour brochure.

Draft 2
Cottages sleeping 2 to 6 people. Autumn short breaks available from £50 per night. Themed weekends during October and November.

Draft 3
Beautifully furnished cottages available for autumn breaks. Rural location, ideal for touring West Country. Excellent walking, horse riding. Colour brochure available.

Questions

1. Which of these ads do you prefer?
2. Which one of these ads would best suit their target market?
3. Can you come up with a better version?
4. Think about your own letting proposition. How easy or difficult is it to get your message over in 20 words?

Local newspapers

Inevitably, once you start advertising, you will be contacted by phone by sales reps from local and regional newspapers trying to sell you space. Often, these papers cover a limited geographical area, so unless you have links with that area, it is difficult to see how you can choose one paper over another. In practice, ask yourself how many people book holidays through a local paper and look carefully at the cost of these ads.

Don't ignore your own local newspaper. Although this may sound odd at first, it is always worthwhile considering some local presence. Many people who live in holiday areas need to put people up in summer, or for weddings for example, and local businesses may need to accommodate staff and visitors.

Magazines

There is a huge range of magazines, from upmarket, mass circulation publications down to very small, special-interest journals. In their favour, magazines have a longer shelf life than newspapers and may be read by a series of people as the magazine is passed around, but they do have longer publication lead times.

● What sort of activities do your target customers undertake, for example walking, riding or surfing? Is there a magazine targeted at those people that would be appropriate for you to advertise in?

● Is it worth advertising in a magazine that specialises in holidays? The advantage is that people read this type of publication with holidays in mind and so there is little 'wasted' advertising. The disadvantage is that you may be competing with many other holiday offerings, thus diluting the impact of your advertising.

Always look at the other advertisements in a magazine. Would your ad look out of place? Is there any point in running your ad for upmarket lodges in a magazine that primarily advertises caravan holidays, for example? Always consider the number of advertisements. Too few, and people may not think of looking there for holidays; too many and you'll be competing for attention.

Many magazines are not sold through newsagents but are distributed through shops or to employees or members of associations. These can be useful, as advertising in these types of magazines can be relatively cheap. They may also give you the opportunity, for example, to offer special discounts to employees or members of associations to help fill shoulder weeks.

Listings of magazines are given in the *BRAD Media Guide*, *Willings*

Press Guide and the *Benn Media Directory*, all of which should be available at reference libraries.

If you intend to place a regular series of advertisements, consider contacting an advertising agency that specialises in the tourism sector. They will be able to achieve higher discounts than you could negotiate individually, and as specialists in the sector, they should also be able to give advice on the best publications to suit your needs.

Whether you are working through an advertising agency or on your own, don't be persuaded to take out more advertising that you think you need or to make hasty decisions based on 'special offers' which you have to sign up for immediately.

Annual publications

Local tourist guides
All tourist areas produce annual guides. These in turn are advertised in a variety of newspapers and magazines, with potential visitors either writing or ringing for a copy or completing a card.

Contact your regional tourist board for details of local guides, the English Tourism Council for guides for the UK market and the British Tourism Authority for publications aimed at overseas guests.

Other commercial guides
Annual commercial guides can be effective. There is a whole range, some general, some location-specific and some tied to special interests and needs (for example pets, children, activity holidays).

Before you sign up check which major booksellers and other outlets are going to stock the guides and when they will be available. You want the books to be in stores at the beginning of January when people are thinking about booking a holiday.

Advantages:

- long shelf life – can generate bookings for many years (particularly when stocked in libraries);

- relatively inexpensive.

Disadvantages:

- long lead times – usually orders need to be placed in the previous summer;

- some guides are more effective than others – do your research before signing up.

Tourist Information Centres

Many local TICs carry advertising for accommodation in their area. It may be worth putting a card in the TIC office, although this is less effective for self-catering operators than it is for bed and breakfast and hotel operators as very few people looking for a holiday let arrive in a tourist destination without having booked in advance.

However, they can be useful for last-minute bookings, for guests to an area thinking of returning the following year or for off-season breaks. Some TICS are now moving to computerised enquiry services positioned at motorway services and other locations en route to the holiday destination. Again, these are probably of limited interest for holiday let operators who do relatively little business this way.

Using pictures

Whether you are talking about a card in a window or an advertisement in a guidebook, there's no doubt that a picture is worth a thousand words. People want to see your units, not read about them – they can read the details later, after they've decided that they like the look of your property.

In many cases, the use of photos in newspaper advertisements, for example, will be prohibitively expensive. But in guidebooks, you will be able to include illustrations at a reasonable cost. Look at the publication carefully before you submit illustrations: in newsprint and in some poor paper quality guides a clear, black and white line drawing can look much more effective than a smudgy colour photo, whereas on glossy paper, a colour photo will look far better.

Unless you are a very accomplished amateur, you should engage a professional photographer. If you do decide to do your own photography, bear in mind the following:

- 35mm colour transparencies will give much better quality than prints and are more widely acceptable to magazines.

- You will probably need to take many shots before you get something good enough to use. Experiment with times of day, angles, different lighting and equipment.

● Take account of timing: although you may want some autumn or spring scenes, most of your publicity material will require summer shots. Carry a camera with you so that you can take advantage of things as they occur.

● Spend time staging your photographs. Flowers and a bottle of wine on the table, children stroking the horses, a couple walking their dog through your grounds, all will help sell your holiday lets. The more you can show people enjoying themselves, the better.

● Good interior shots are very difficult to achieve due to limited space and poor lighting – this may well be the time to call in a professional.

Making contact

Having seen your advertisement, a potential guest must be able to reach you easily for more information. This means considering whether to publish phone, fax and/or e-mail numbers.

Contacting you by phone
If you're using one telephone line for home and business, make sure that all members of the family answer the phone in a polite way, giving the name of the establishment. You never know when a potential guest may ring.

Consider where the phone is located: somewhere quiet is essential, as you don't want to have to compete with the TV, radio and your children in the background. Make sure all availability details and tariffs are by the phone, together with a note pad and pen.

Use a call minding service or answerphone when you aren't there.

Contacting you by fax
Usually it is far better to have personal contact with an enquirer – it gives you the chance to find out exactly what the guest is looking for, and to present yourselves in a professional, friendly way. It also gives a voice to your operation.

But a fax can be useful, particularly for overseas enquirers, who may be more comfortable with written than spoken English. It can also be useful for late bookings, where confirmations, directions and so on can be quickly exchanged. If you are going to give out a fax number, then the fax must be available at all times.

Contacting you by e-mail

This is becoming more and more popular for initial brochure requests. Make sure that you check your e-mail at least once a day and preferably more frequently – e-mail users expect a quick response.

DESIGNING BROCHURES

Even if they have seen a website, or they know your property already, potential guests usually still require a brochure.

You have various options, from doing the whole thing yourself on a PC through to commissioning a complete design and print service from a professional. Whatever you decide, the first step is to collect brochures from some other operators. Sit down and analyse them: what do you like and why? What do you dislike? What impression does the brochure give? Who does it appear to be targeted at?

Look for colours and colour combinations, layout, number of photos, style of font, size, type of information included in the brochure, style of text and so on. This will start to give you a good idea of what you want for your brochure.

Do-it-yourself brochures

Personal computers have revolutionised what we can do at home. The keys to a successful home-produced brochure are as follows:

- Thinking carefully about the design. The most common problem with home-produced material is 'just because I can'. You can get carried away with all the different fonts, effects and layouts available to the extent that the finished article looks like a complete mess from a design viewpoint – a sure way to mark you out as an amateur.

- Considering the quality of printing that you can achieve. The quality of your pictures is critical to the success of your brochure. Before you decide to go it alone, look at various printers and decide whether the quality of photograph they can print is good enough for your brochure. Similarly, digital cameras or prints scanned into your PC may look good on your screen, but are they of sufficiently high definition and can you print them?

Using photographs

Consider photos of the interiors, exteriors and the local area and tourist spots. If you're not happy with the quality of printing you can achieve, you may want to consider stick-on colour photos, like those used by some estate agents on their details. These can be very effective, but make sure that the weight of paper or card is sufficient to carry the weight of the photos.

You can also use line drawings, and these work especially well as logos or on your letterheads or envelopes. Go for as simple a drawing as possible – you want something that will work at quite a small size. Don't rely on line drawings in your brochure unless you have to – people prefer to see actual photographs, where things cannot easily be omitted or changed.

Writing the words

First, your brochure should be attracting attention and creating desire. Then, you need to be thinking about giving information and filling in the details, and making it easy for your customer to make a booking with you.

Put yourself in the mind of a potential guest. Tell that guest why they should want to holiday with you. What can you offer them? When you are drafting the copy for your brochure:

● keep language clear and simple;

● avoid overblown descriptions;

● stick to the facts;

● use language that is specific and conjures up pictures;

● avoid clichés.

Keep working on your copy until you have something which is interesting and hopefully, a little different from the competition. Don't exaggerate, and be up front about any potential problems.

Printing your brochure

Unless you are taking over an existing business and have access to good information, you will probably not know initially how many brochures to have printed. If you are doing it yourself, you can print more or less on demand. With a full-colour brochure, it may well be that you are limited by the size of a minimum print run, so that your brochure may need to last several seasons; it is always cheaper to have a longer initial print run than to reprint extra copies later on. If this is the case:

● make sure that the information going into your brochure isn't going to change;

● use inserts – either produced yourself or printed – for detailed information and for information that is going to change, primarily tariffs. Save the full-colour, glossy brochure for selling your holidays. Make sure that the whole package doesn't become too bitty, and keep an eye on the overall weight of your package – you don't want to just fall into a higher postage weight band.

Having designed your brochure, make sure that your other stationery items – letter heads, compliment slips, envelopes, standard letters – are of the same design, colour and paper quality and that the whole package works together.

CASE STUDY

George designs his own brochure

George has his own PC and is confident that he can produce a reasonable brochure himself. He decides to use stick on photos and asks a friend who is a keen photographer to take several rolls of film. He drafts out a sample brochure and shows it to friends and also a small business adviser at the local Business Link. He gains valuable feedback from this exercise and amends his brochure accordingly.

The small business adviser looks through George's photographs and suggests that George make better use of the flexibility offered by using stick-on photographs. For example, if George gets an enquiry from the farm holiday guide he is advertising in, he could use a photograph of children on the farm with baby lambs, or if an enquiry comes via a walking guide, George could use a photo of a couple, for example, walking a dog through one of his fields.

George goes back to his photographer friend, and they plan a series of shots showing different activities and so George is able to tailor his brochures at a very low cost.

USING A LETTING AGENCY

Whether to go it alone or work with a letting agency is probably one of the biggest initial decisions you'll have to take.

Often, new owners are advised to go with an agency for the first one or two years, and this may indeed be a condition from some lenders. Initially, you may have little choice, due to the timing of brochure production and buying advertising space.

Reasons for using an agency

● *Timing*. Initially at least you may not have time to organise your own marketing and advertising.

● *Skills*. You may feel that you do not have the skills to undertake your own marketing and advertising. With an agency, the marketing, advertising and bookings are handled for you. All you have to do is prepare your units and cash the cheque that the agency sends you every month.

● *Expense*. If you are a small operator, handling only one cottage for example, organising your own advertising may be too expensive to be a viable option.

● *Time*. Using an agency will save you time answering enquiries, sending out brochures, taking bookings and completing associated paperwork. It also frees up your time during the year. You do not have to be around, for example, in January when all the enquiries for the summer start to come through and you don't need to be at home every day to handle enquiries.

● *Other benefits*. An agency may give you access to other services such as specialised insurance, buying discounts, holiday home exchange schemes and accounting advice.

Disadvantages of using an agency

● *Cost*. The difference between what the customer pays and what you receive can be quite substantial and is likely to vary at different times of the year.

● *Loss of control*. The agency may well specify certain conditions, for example detailing the inventory you need to provide, or requiring changes to the layout of your units.

- *Loss of personal contact.* You lose the opportunity to sell your properties to people, to explain exactly your facilities and to deal with any special requirements on a personal level.

- *Loss of value for money for customers.* Consider what potential guests will pay for their holiday. For example, a small operator will operate below the VAT threshold so bookings through an agency will automatically be 17.5 per cent more expensive on top of the agency commission. Add to this the possibility of compulsory insurance and you have a guest potentially paying quite a lot more for his holiday, which in turn might mean increased expectations or a perception of an expensive holiday which you have to then deal with.

- *Loss of flexibility.* If you are running units yourself you are able to react to circumstances, for example adjusting prices for a slow selling period or increasing advertising for a special event or a particular timeframe – this flexibility is lost if you are using an agent.

Choosing an agency

Most agencies will send you an information pack and will offer to send someone round to talk to you. Some things to consider are as follows:

- Do they guarantee a minimum number of weeks?

- Do they charge a registration fee?

- Do they quote average occupancy figures? A common complaint is that agencies will fill peak school holiday weeks (i.e. the easy weeks) but do less well during the shoulder and off-peak times.

- How do they advertise their brochures? When do they appear? Are they stocked in travel agents? Do guests have to pay for a brochure?

- Can you take you own bookings? Is there any limit on the number of weeks that you can book yourself in the high and off-peak seasons?

- How do they discount late bookings? Do they make special efforts to sell cancelled weeks?

- What additional support do they offer – legal and financial advice, discounts on goods and services for example?

- Do you like their brochure? Is it attractive and easy to read? Are the photographs or drawings of good quality? How many other units are in the brochure – these are your competitors – and how will people choose you over all the others?

Using a local agency

These deal with a specific geographical area, and thus have the advantage of being more focused. They tend to be smaller operations, thus offering a more personal service. Some local agencies also take on the management of properties, organising everything including cleaning and maintenance.

MAKING THE INTERNET WORK FOR YOU

There has been a remarkable growth in the number of bookings and enquiries made over the Internet, with a corresponding fall in the number of bookings taken through traditional media. It can be a very cost-effective option for operators, particularly small operators who find traditional advertising media expensive.

The Internet can provide great benefits to buyers of holidays.

- They can get as much, and usually more, information than they get from a brochure.

- They can have a good look at a property before they make contact.

- They can search for any specific requirements, locations or facilities.

- They can do all this at a time that suits them, and get information immediately, rather than looking at a property, phoning up, either getting through or leaving a message, then waiting for a brochure to arrive in the post.

- They can get up-to-the-minute information from a well-run website regarding availability, latest prices and special offers.

There are a range of options available to operators, from designing and operating their own web-site to having a presence on someone else's site, without even having a computer. Most people will fall in between, relying on some outside help to set up and manage their own website.

Building your own website

While details of how to build a website are outside the scope of this book, some principles are as follows:

Layout and design
All the rules of good layout and design are relevant here, perhaps more so, as there is the opportunity to add all kinds of gimmicks – sound, moving banners, video and so on – which can make your site look messy if you're not careful. Keep it clear, keep it simple, and keep it coherent in terms of style.

Visual information
Take advantage of the opportunity to add lots of pictures. But load times are an important factor – make sure that any graphics don't slow the site to an extent that users get bored waiting for it to load. They'll just move on somewhere else.

Making contact
Make sure that it is clear how to contact you – make contact details prominent and clear, whether by phone, fax or e-mail. If you publish an e-mail address for enquiries, then make sure that you check your mail regularly. People expect very quick responses from e-mail – it's no good going in once a week to check.

Make it easy to use
Make sure the site is easy to navigate – don't leave users wandering, unsure of how to get to the right piece of information.

Publicising your site
A site is only as good as its links – make sure that the site is linked as widely as possible, that key words are relevant and up to date and that the site is regularly submitted to search engines. Use the website address on your letterheads and other stationery, and publish it in any guide-books you advertise in.

Keeping the site up to date
The whole point of websites is that you can have something up to the minute with latest availability, special offers and what's on soon. There's nothing worse than a site containing out of date information.

Keep well back from the leading edge

There's little point in having facilities that only work with the most up-to-date software – it's more than likely that your customers won't have this level of technology. Always remember that you're selling cottages, not websites.

Getting someone to build you a site

There is a lot of advice and training available on using the Internet and building sites. Before you approach anyone to build you a site, it's advisable to get some advice and do your research first. The more you understand about the way websites work, the better you'll be able to specify exactly what you want.

There are many, many people offering to build websites. As with any type of work, if possible, go by personal recommendation from other operators in the same business.

Some practical tips

Don't rely on statistics from the web builder or host regarding the number of 'hits'. i.e. visits to a particular site. Talk to the owners and find out the actual number of enquiries and bookings originating from the website compared to other sources.

Talk about what the charge includes. What happens if the site crashes? What about updating information – how often, what charge, what response time?

Make sure that whoever is building your site understands the sort of business you are in. Some web designers are technically very good but lack the business background that you need.

If you don't have a PC

Even if you don't have a PC, it is possible to have a listing on either a tourist board site or an equivalent commercial site. What you lose is the ability to include lots of information and the immediacy of a potential guest being able to contact you by e-mail or to find out more information about your business by linking through to a site operated by you. In general, guests will either make contact by phoning or faxing you, or they may e-mail a central number which in turn generates a fax enquiry to you.

As a tourism operator, you will soon find that there are many organisations offering websites or website listings: do your homework before you sign up with any of these. More useful is the fact that many guide books are now operating their own sites, with free listings for those people already listed in their guides: these free-of-charge options are well worth taking up, but make sure that you are not committed to paying for a listing on their website at some future date.

CASE STUDY

Sue decides to go online

As a very small operator, Sue's advertising budget is limited. She decides to look at the possibilities of the Internet; she already has a PC and is familiar with the Internet. She believes that she will make the most of her advertising if she can link her site into the main tourism accommodation site for the area. She also wants to tap into the local business market, and knows that if she wants to attract corporate clients, she must be fluent in using e-mail.

She is able to get a grant towards helping learn more about website design: she wants to have control of the site herself, and in the future she thinks she may be able to use the knowledge she is gaining to offer a similar, tailored service to other operators of holiday flats, possibly setting up a website to advertise accommodation in the town.

She builds her own website, finding it easier than she had imagined, and soon finds that e-mail enquiries are coming through.

ASSESSING THE EFFECTIVENESS OF YOUR MARKETING

Whatever form of marketing and advertising you undertake, you will inevitably find that some things work better than others. Keep proper records of where your bookings originate from and from this calculate cost per booking for each type of advertising. A relatively cheap initial outlay will not be cost-effective if it doesn't generate bookings in sufficient quantity.

Some practical tips

● It is good practice to ask enquirers where they heard about your advert. Track this monthly.

● Don't forget to count returning visitors – you should be aiming to get as many people coming back as possible.

● Don't forget to count referrals – word of mouth is the most effective form of advertising.

● Don't forget that an entry in a guidebook may have a shelf life of several years, either in someone's home or on the library shelf.

● Think about putting a space on your booking form for 'where you heard about us' – in case you didn't pick it up from their phone call.

It can be difficult to track information if you have a presence on more than one website, for example, or if people contact you via e-mail and your e-mail address is published in several places. The really interesting information you need – how people searching the web initially come across your site, using which key words and which search engine, is difficult to determine without specialist software.

If you are taking a lot of enquiries to an answerphone or voice mail system, as well as asking enquirers to talk clearly and spell out their name and address, ask them also to state where they heard about you.

If people are writing in response to an advertisement, again ask them to indicate where they heard about you. It is possible to include a marker in the address you quote which will indicate the source of the enquiry, for example 'Dept ST' for an advertisement in the *Sunday Times*, although this could be seen as being a bit hackneyed.

Keeping statistics

Think about tracking for each type of advertising:

● number of enquiries;

● number of bookings;

● conversion rate, e.g. percentage of enquiries converted to bookings;

● advertising cost per booking.

Conversion rate is particularly interesting. If you are generating a high number of enquires to a low number of bookings, something is wrong that needs looking at.

Keep an eye on changes in your figures, month on month, and also compare the same period in the current and previous years. Why have things changed?

Above all, act on these statistics. If cost per booking is high, then you have two options:

● change your advertisement – the copy, the photographs, the layout or size – or

● drop your advertisement in this medium altogether and spend the money elsewhere.

You will want to give any particular advertisement a fair chance, particularly a classified advertisement, but don't hang on when it is clear that the ad isn't generating enough business for you.

Inherently, some types of advertising are more expensive. For example, some 'emergency' Sunday newspaper advertising to fill a slow couple of weeks will have a high cost, but it may well be better than the alternative, which is having the units lie empty when they could be earning some income.

CHECKLIST

● Start defining the type of brochure and promotional material you need.

● Start looking at different advertising media and comparing the costs of advertising in each.

● Assess whether you will use a letting agency, and if so, start comparing their services.

● Think seriously about exploiting the Internet – and seek help or training if you need it.

7

Running the Business

So your property is ready and your advertising is in place. Now is the time to actually deal with taking bookings, to start welcoming your first guests and to get on with running the business.

KEEPING PAPERWORK UNDER CONTROL

You must be very organised with your paperwork and set up a good filing system straightaway. Your records of guest bookings must be complete and accurate.

Using a computer will greatly increase the information you can store, but if you do this make sure that you do frequent back-ups and that you maintain some form of paper record of bookings in case of emergencies. Also make sure that you are familiar with the principles of the Data Protection Act.

Enquiry Details

You will need some way of capturing enquiry details. For phone messages, something along the lines shown in Figure 11 is suggested.

Enquiry log

If you're handling a large number of enquiries, you may find it useful to keep a separate log for quick reference and summarising statistics (see Figure 12).

Booking chart

You will need a booking chart, telling you immediately what is available when (see Figure 13). It can be a wall chart, which is easy to see but only

Customer Enquiry Form

Date:

Name: ....

Address: ....

....

Town: ....

County: ....

Postcode: ....

Telephone no: .... Fax no: ....

E-mail no: ....

Size of party? Adults .... Children .... Dogs ....

Particular dates? .... Particular unit? ....

Heard about us from:
Website ❑ Tourist Info Centre ❑
Guide Book 1 ❑ Guide Book 2 ❑
Advert 1 ❑ Advert 2 ❑

Notes ....

....

....

Brochure sent out on ....

Fig. 11.   A sample enquiry form.

useful if you deal with all your bookings in one place. It is much easier to have your chart on a large sheet of paper that you can carry around if you need to.

In the example shown in Figure 13, provisional bookings awaiting the return of a booking form and deposit are shown in italics (Thomas) – in your booking chart, you may want to pencil these in. On confirmation, the names are inked in and a '/' put by their name to indicate that a

Enquiry Date	Name	Source	Dates	Party size	Booking?
2 Jan	Mrs Smith	Website	August	2 ad 2 child	
2 Jan	Mr Thomas	Local holiday guide	7–14 June	4 ad	Y
3 Jan	Jane Paul	*AB Magazine* Jan issue	Easter	*2–4 ad?* + dog short break	
4 Jan	Mrs Edwards	Website	Spring	2 ad 2 child	Provisional

Fig. 12. A sample enquiry log.

Booking Chart Extract for Year 200X			
Week starting	**Rose Cottage**	**Jasmine Cottage**	**Bluebell Cottage**
10/7	Jones X		
17/7	Jones X		Smith X
24/7		Edwards /	
31/7			
7/8	*Thomas*	*Thomas*	
14/8			
21/8			

Fig. 13. A sample booking chart.

deposit has been paid. (Edwards). On payment of the final amount, the '/' is made into a 'X' (Jones, Smith). Although you will keep detailed payment records elsewhere, this does have the advantage of showing the status of all your bookings at a glance.

Customer details

Your booking chart needs to be backed up by detailed customer records. You will have received a booking form. In addition to this, you need to capture the following:

Payment details:

- date deposit confirmed;

- date and amount of final payment due;

- date and amount of final payment received;

- where necessary, dates and details of outstanding payments chased and any other correspondence.

Special requirements:

- cots, highchairs or other items required;

- requests for groceries, milk or newspapers;

- unusual arrival times.

All notes of customer details should be filed per unit, in date order and archived once the holiday has been taken.

You will be unlikely to hold enough cots, high chairs or other items that you provide on request to equip all units simultaneously. If this is the case, keep a record somewhere of the number of these items required per week so that you know well in advance whether you need to beg, borrow or buy for any week where demand exceeds your stock.

Standard letters

As well as normal business stationery, letter headed paper, compliment slips, envelopes and booking forms, you will also need standard letters for:

- acknowledgement of receipt of deposit;

- acknowledgement of receipt of final payment;

- reminders for overdue amounts.

Collecting statistics

Keep a summary of your bookings each month, then you can see at a glance who has booked in which unit and the source of the booking. At the end of the month, you will want to collate some basic information, and then as you progress, you will want to compare year-on-year progress.

CASE STUDY

Fiona and Michael start to collect their statistics

Mid-way through their first season, Fiona and Michael realise that unless they start to keep some statistics on a regular basis, they will have a huge job at the end of the season going back to draw out the relevant information. They decide to lay out a format for the information they want to look at, and then use this format on an ongoing basis for year-on-year comparisons.

They end up with one sheet analysing enquiries, and one sheet looking at bookings. Their booking analysis for the first six months is shown in Figure 14.

Questions

1. How useful is this format?
2. Is there any additional information you'd like to see included?
3. Having separate sheets for bookings and enquiries could be cumbersome. How could you incorporate the information onto one sheet and still make it easy to read?
4. How are you going to lay out your marketing statistics?
5. How well are bookings going? What, if any, remedial action is needed?

SURVIVING CHANGEOVER DAY

If all goes well, your changeover day will run smoothly. Things can and do go wrong, though. For example:

- not all your guests leave on time;

- staff go sick or are late;

- new guests arrive early;

- a unit is left in a very poor condition so that a major clean is required;

- something is broken or needs replacing that you didn't know about.

Booking Analysis – January to June 200X

	Jan	Feb	Mar	Apr	May	June	July	Aug	Sept	Oct	Nov	Dec	Total	Cost of ad/£	Actual cost per booking	Target cost per booking
Tourist Info	1												1	70	70.00	
Guide Book A	1	4	3	2	1	2							13	250	19.23	
Guide Book B	1	2	1	1		2							7	150	21.43	
Magazine A	1	3	1		1								6	342	57.00	
Magazine B	2			1		1							3	120	30.00	
Freidns/family		1		1		1							3	0	–	
Referrals														0	–	
Previous guest														0	–	
Local visitor														0	–	
Unknown			1										1	0	–	
															–	
															–	
Total	5	10	6	5	3	6							35	932	26.63	10

Number of weeks booked

	Jan	Feb	Mar	Apr	May	June	July	Aug	Sept	Oct	Nov	Dec	Total	Target weeks for year
Cottage 1	2	4	3	2	1	2							14	16
Cottage 2	1	3	1	1		1							7	16
Cottage 3	1	1		1									3	16
Cottage 4				1	1	1							3	16
Cottage 5	2	4	2		1	2							11	16
Total	6	12	6	5	3	6							38	80

Other targets

	Actual	Target
Two week bookings	3	10
Overseas bookings	2	10
Friends/referrals/return guests	3	10

Fig. 14. Sample booking statistics

Some practical tips

Cleaners
Make sure that your cleaning staff are properly trained. Take them on for a few trial sessions and work with them, particularly if they have no experience of this type of work. Make sure that they understand exactly what is expected. Many people think that anyone can do this work. In practice, it takes stamina, speed, an eye for detail and a lot of elbow grease to get a holiday let thoroughly cleaned and prepared.

It is possible to allow a certain time, say three hours, for cleaning a unit. The danger with this is that the full allowance might be taken but this is no guarantee of quality so supervision or checking is required.

Be prepared
Do as much as possible in advance, for example making sure that:

● linen is sorted by unit;

● cleaning kits are ready and waiting;

● provisions – toilet rolls, bin bags, kitchen towels, etc. – are all sorted and ready;

● you have spares of most items – glasses, crockery, teapots – to hand for emergencies.

If guests leave early, try to make sure that someone can get in and make a start on cleaning.

Guests
Encourage guests to tell you of any problems during the week. If these can't be fixed during their stay at least you know what you need to fit into your changeover day.

If you want your units to be in a reasonable state when guests leave:

● hand them over in a pristine state – the better kept a property is, the more likely it is that guests will look after it;

● provide cleaning materials, vacuum cleaners, brooms and bin bags for guests' use;

● think about ease of use and cleaning when you're planning – little things like somewhere to put dirty shoes and boots near the entrance can make all the difference when it comes to cleaning up.

If you have a large number of units, it may well be worthwhile staggering changeovers on, say, a Friday and Saturday. Obviously, if you do this, you need to make sure that guests staying over on changeover day aren't inconvenienced.

STAYING ON TOP OF MAINTENANCE

As soon as you are full, there is no chance for maintenance to be carried out. Emergency maintenance is limited to a few snatched hours on changeover day, or emergency repairs during a guest's stay.

The key to maintenance, as with everything else, is planning. Time and trouble spent keeping on top of maintenance is well worthwhile. What you want to avoid are minor problems building up into major ones.

Some practical tips

● Have a schedule of work, especially if you have several units, and keep a note of when each item of work is done. It can be very easy to lose track. Make a schedule of things that need checking regularly, for example electrical appliances.

● Keep an eye open during changeover day for small jobs that need doing and encourage your staff to do the same.

● Use easy-clean surfaces, for example vinyl paint on the walls. Make sure that you make a note of paint colours and brands used in each room, and keep a spare can ready for emergency touching up.

● Fitting in exterior work is often a battle against the elements and the short days of winter. Use every opportunity to get this work done when the weather allows. Interior work can be fitted in at other times.

● Have a list of people that you can call on in emergencies for jobs that you can't tackle yourself. Build up a relationship with them so that you can get urgent jobs done quickly without being charged the earth.

REVIEWING YOUR FINANCES

You will need some sort of financial control system in place when you start business. In practice this means:

- having a means of recording income and expenditure from which your accounts can be prepared;

- regularly monitoring cash flow and keeping on top of payments to suppliers and money due in from guests;

- reconciling bank accounts to ensure that everything is being correctly recorded.

You'll also need to deal with National Insurance Contributions and PAYE for your employees, account for VAT if you're registered and pay your own National Insurance Contributions and income tax liabilities.

The sophistication of your financial system will depend on the size and complexity of your business, but if you have a computer:

- consider using a proprietary package for logging and analysing income and expenditure;

- use a spreadsheet for tracking progress against budget.

Keeping records

You may well find that you need to use an accountant to prepare your year-end accounts and to help with your tax return. The sort of information you will need to provide includes:

- letting income for the year, letting agent's statements, other income (electricity, meals etc), money owed to you at the year end (debtors);

- details of expenditure, cash payments, capital equipment purchased or sold during the year, money owed by you at the year end (creditors);

- copies of bank statements, cheque stubs, paying in stubs, receipts, mortgage interest statements, bank interest paid and received;

- copies of previous years' accounts, details of tax paid during the year, VAT accounts;

- details of the allocation of shared costs between business and personal use, for example, for cars, computers, telephone charges or using of part of your home as an office.

In addition, if this is the first year of trading:

● details of the purchase price and any goodwill or fixtures and fittings;

● improvements made to the fabric of the buildings, capital items purchased;

● details of any of your own furniture or equipment transferred into the business.

CASE STUDY

George does his accounts

At the end of the tax year, George goes to the accountant he has always used in the past with a box full of receipts and his bank statements. He has assumed that the accountant will be able to do his holiday let accounts at the same time as the smallholding business, and that as a result, the accountant's fees will not be very much more.

The accountant hasn't been involved in George's new venture. He gives George a list of all the supplementary information he needs, and as there is a lot of work to do sorting out the accounts, the fee he quotes is considerably higher than George expected.

George realises that he should have consulted his accountant first and set up a system for collecting information himself that would have kept the workload, and the fees, down.

Measuring progress against budget

You will need to monitor whether your income and expenditure are in line with expectations on an ongoing basis:

● If not, why not?

● Do your forecasts need adjusting as a result?

● What are the implications of an over/underspend?

● Do you need to take any actions as a result (either cutting costs or increasing bookings)?

In financial terms, you are comparing actual against budget. The difference is the variance: a positive variance if results are better than plan, or a negative variance if results are worse.

Completing a bank reconciliation

The purpose of a bank reconciliation is to match your records to your bank statement. You need to adjust for timing differences, for example cheques that you show as paid in will not show on your bank statement until they are cleared.

An example
Fiona and Michael's first bank statement indicates that they have £5,002 in the bank, whereas they expected to see a figure of £4,765. After looking through their accounts, they draw up the following bank reconciliation:

Our closing balance at 31 March	4,765	as recorded in our books
Less cheques paid in not cleared	(25)	income paid in but hasn't appeared yet on statement
Plus cheques not yet presented	60	cheques written but not yet presented
Plus other items:		
transfer direct to bank	200	deposit from overseas guest paid directly into bank a/c
interest	2	interest generated on balance
Equals closing balance as reported by the bank	5,002	

CHECKLIST

- Design the process you'll use for recording bookings and set up the necessary paperwork and files.

- Look at what information you want to collect in order to compile statistics.

- Set up a maintenance plan.

- Set up a system for recording and reviewing your finances.

8

Asking the Experts

Before you start to trade you must have a very clear idea of the regulatory framework in which you are operating, particularly in the area of safety legislation. This chapter will initially deal with safety legislation, and then move on to other regulatory areas that you need to be aware of.

This chapter aims to give an overview only of the current situation. It is your responsibility to investigate these areas in detail, ensuring that you have the most up-to-date information possible.

If you are working with a booking agency, you will find that they will give advice on these issues and may impose their own safety requirements and recommendations over and above what is required by law.

LOOKING AT SAFETY LEGISLATION

The best source of information is the Pink Booklet, produced by the English Tourism Council, and available by post or online.

The booklet gives a review of the legislation affecting both serviced and self-catering accommodation. A list of the main items is given here, together with information on where to go for further help. This section covers regulations relating to self-catering operations; note that additional regulations apply to bed and breakfast and other serviced accommodation and to other activities, such as the preparation and sale of food.

Contact details for all the organisations listed in this chapter are given in 'Useful Addresses' at the end of this book.

Safety legislation

Gas Safety
There are extensive regulations governing the installation and maintenance of gas supplies and appliances, the aim being to prevent carbon monoxide poisoning. Of particular relevance are the requirements to have appliance safety checks carried out yearly and for work on gas

appliances to be carried out by CORGI-approved fitters. Note that many of the regulations apply to liquid petroleum gas (LPG) as well as natural gas.

Further information is available from the Health and Safety Executive. Publications are available from HSE books, and advice can be obtained from the Gas Safety Action Line on 0800 300 363.

Electricity

There is conflicting advice as to whether holiday properties are regarded as places of work and therefore covered by the Electricity at Work Regulations or not. Whatever the case, basically, all electrical equipment and systems must be safe. Although there are at the time of writing no specific recommendations on a testing, service or maintenance regime, it is strongly recommended that a formal testing procedure is in place.

Further information is available from the Health and Safety Executive (Electricity at Work Regulations), local authority trading standards departments (Electrical Equipment Safety Regulations) and the DTI.

Fire precautions

You will not normally need a fire certificate for self-catering accommodation. You will, however, need to comply with regulations covering fire resistance standards for furniture. You should always look for appropriate labels before buying furniture and furnishings. The regulations cover ignitability tests for beds, divans, mattresses, seating and sofas, scatter cushions and pillows.

Further information is available from the DTI and local authority trading standards departments.

Health and Safety at Work

You have a duty of care to your employees. The chances are that you would do what is required as a matter of course; the responsibility is on the employer to assess and manage any risks to employees from their work activities.

Further information is available from the Health and Safety Executive and local environmental health officers.

General Product Safety Regulations

Items that you provide for guest use must be safe. Provide instructions for items where they are needed; check and ensure that everything is in good working order and that potential hazards are dealt with.

Further advice is available from the DTI and local authority trading standards departments.

Safety of guests
Proprietors are liable for the safety of everyone who comes onto their premises. Again, this is primarily a matter of good housekeeping, covering areas such as good lighting and the provision of well-maintained, safe, fixtures and fittings.

Swimming pools and gyms
A number of fatal accidents have triggered growing concern regarding the safety of swimming pools. You have an obligation under health and safety legislation to ensure that your guests are not exposed to risks. *Safety in Swimming Pools* published by the Sports Council gives advice regarding appropriate safety notices, but you are very strongly advised to seek advice from local environmental health officers on how you should operate these types of facility as the current trend is towards much stricter control.

Other legislation

Planning permission
You may need planning permission for:

● internal alterations which affect the exterior of a building;

● new buildings;

● change of use;

● outdoor advertisements;

● fencing, in certain circumstances.

This is not a complete list, and an initial consultation with your local planning department will clarify what you may need to do.

Private water supplies
Regulations cover the sampling and testing of private water supplies.
Further information is available from local environmental health officers.

Resale of electricity
This applies to metering where guests are charged separately for their own consumption. There is a maximum amount that can be charged based on units consumed plus a daily availability charge, designed to cover installation and standing charges.

Further information is available from electricity suppliers or OFGEM (Office of Gas and Electricity Markets).

TV licences
If televisions are provided for guest use, it is the owner's responsibility to organise a TV licence. The Hotel Comprehensive Licence is available to self-catering property owners providing that there are two or more units available at the same site or within the same premises (if you live across the road, you will need another licence). It is not currently possible to obtain these licences from post offices.

Further information is available from the Manual Licensing Centre, Bristol.

Trade Descriptions Act
In your brochure or promotional literature, you must not make false statements about the services, facilities or location of the accommodation you offer.

Further information is available from local trading standards departments.

Guest registration
For guests over the age of 16, you must have a record of their full name and nationality. In addition, for guests who are not British, Commonwealth or Republic of Ireland citizens, you are also required to keep a record of their passport number and place of issue and details of their next destination.

Other areas of legislation
Other areas you may need to research are:

- food safety – further information is available from local environmental health departments and MAFF;

- outdoor safety for adventure activities for the under 18s – further information is available from the Health and Safety Executive;

- liquor licensing – further information is available from the local Clerk to the Justices;

- Data Protection Act – further information is available from the Data Protection Registrar;

- employment legislation.

CASE STUDY

Sue is offered some furniture

One of Sue's friends, hearing about her new venture, offers her some furniture that she no longer needs. Although in very good condition, Sue cannot find any fire resistance labels on the sofa and matching chairs. A chaise longue, which Sue's friend was told was Edwardian when she purchased it, should be useable as pre-1950 items are exempt from the regulations, but as Sue has no proof of the date of manufacture, she has to decline this and the other upholstered items.

Sue's friend also offers her a toaster and kettle, again in very good condition. Sue cannot rely on the safety of these items; she has no operating instructions or manufacturer's details, and the items do not carry a CE mark, so she decides to err on the side of caution and buy new items.

UNDERSTANDING TAX

This is a very simple introduction to some of the different types of tax you may encounter.

Income tax and corporation tax

The type of tax that you pay on income or profits will depend on the form of business that you operate under. Most holiday let businesses are run by individuals operating as sole traders or by partnerships, in which case you will pay normal income tax on your profits. You will submit your accounts as part of your self-assessment. You will also be responsible for paying your own weekly, flat-rate Class 2 National Insurance Contributions if your earnings exceed the lower earnings limit and also possibly Class 4 Contributions which are based on a percentage of profits.

If your business is a limited company, the situation will be a little more complicated and you will be liable for income tax on your salary and the company will pay corporation tax on profits. Directors of limited companies are liable to pay National Insurance Contributions, and the company will pay employer contributions for those directors.

The Inland Revenue produce a series of leaflets – see the 'Further Reading' section at the end of this book.

Employee taxes

If you employ staff, you are responsible for collecting income tax through the PAYE system, for deducting National Insurance Contributions and for paying employer's contributions, providing the lower earnings limit is exceeded.

Again, the Inland Revenue can provide a lot of advice in this area and in many areas they provide local training seminars for new employers.

Capital gains tax

This is a tax on the profit you make when you sell your business. There are allowances and reliefs available, for example on retirement, and you will need to contact the Inland Revenue for the latest position or an accountant for advice on how CGT will impact on you.

VAT

You must register your business for VAT if your turnover exceeds the current threshold. Once you are VAT registered, you must charge VAT on the supply of your accommodation. At the end of each quarter, the amount due to the Customs & Excise is the VAT that you have collected, less the VAT that you have paid on goods and services purchased for your business.

CASE STUDY

Fiona and Michael employ staff

Fiona and Michael have never employed any staff themselves and are worried about the tax and National Insurance implications. They contact their local tax office, who in turn pass them onto the new employer helpline. After taking their details, the helpline despatches the relevant forms and documents.

However, when Fiona receives these, she panics at the volume of paper that has arrived. She phones the helpline again, and someone goes through what she needs to do. She finds it much easier than she thought, and soon has a system up and running for paying her staff, deducting tax and National Insurance and for making payments to the Inland Revenue.

The helpline phone her to see how she is getting on and she is able to iron out a few problems. She also takes advantage of a free seminar organised by the local tax office for new employers which goes through the things she needs to do at the end of the tax year.

ENSURING YOU'RE INSURED

It is well worth taking the time to discuss your insurance requirements with a broker – they will be able to give detailed advice about the potential risks that you may face. Alternatively, many letting agencies are able to offer insurance packages designed specifically for holiday lets.

Public liability insurance

Public liability insurance covers civil actions brought by visitors who sustain an injury on your property. Unlike employers' liability insurance, there is no statutory requirement to take out public liability insurance. It is, however, strongly recommended and is a prerequisite for entry into the English Tourism Council quality standard system.

Employers' liability insurance

There is a statutory requirement for employers to insure against legal claims for injury or disease of employees arising from their employment. A copy of the certificate should be displayed at the place of business and a copy must be available for inspection. The policy must be placed with an authorised insurer.

Other insurance

- Buildings and contents

- Loss of rental income

- Cancellation insurance

- Personal accident and health insurance

- Key-man insurance

- Motor vehicle insurance – do you need business cover?

Most other types of insurance are, in theory, optional, but you would want, for example, to take out buildings insurance. Indeed, this is more than likely to be a condition of any loan that you have on a property.

With a small business, you need to think very carefully about what would happen if you or your partner was sick for any length of time. Would you be able to keep the business afloat? Would it survive – at what financial cost? Health, personal accident and/or key-man insurance may be appropriate.

CHECKLIST

- Research the current legal and regulatory environment that applies to your business.

- Contact the Inland Revenue to discuss your tax position and that of your staff.

- Make sure that you have appropriate and adequate insurance cover.

9

Keeping on Track

REVIEWING PROGRESS

Things you'll need to look at regularly are:

- your financial position – especially cash flow;

- bookings and enquiries – how they are progressing, what's working well and what isn't;

- payments – making sure that payments are coming through at the due dates;

- the longer term – are you likely to meet your targets for income and expenditure this year? What is your likely position for future years?

It is also worthwhile doing the following:

- If you are a partnership, make sure that you know who has responsibility for monitoring various aspects of your business results. Don't fall into debt because you both assumed the other person was keeping check of the finances!

- Whatever the size of your operation, make sure that you sit down and have a proper review session, say once a month. Do you need to do any extra promotions? Are there any problem areas that need to be tackled? What is your plan of work for the coming weeks?

- Try to keep the business plan as a working document. Review progress against that plan and update it as necessary.

Don't assume that if everything is currently going to plan, this situation will necessarily continue. All holiday let operators will tell you that they have good and bad years, and that sometimes it's impossible to determine why. What you can do, though, is keep ahead of the game. What changes are happening to the local area, to the tourism sector as a whole and to the economy that may affect your business? What changes can you exploit to your benefit? How are customer expectations changing? One thing is certain – you can't afford to stand still.

COPING WITH SETBACKS AND MAKING CHANGES

Every business suffers setbacks. Don't allow a setback to become a major crisis – be aware and be realistic about what is happening. Early action is vital to bring things back on course. Ignoring a situation rarely does anything except make things worse in the long run.

It can be very difficult to be objective when the business is your own, but this is something you have to work at. Think critically about what has gone wrong, particularly the assumptions you made in your plans, and build this experience into your future plans so that you don't make the same mistakes again.

DEALING WITH FINANCIAL PROBLEMS

If you're not making as much money as you anticipated, the first step is to look back at your original plans and try to determine which factor or combination of factors is at work.

Looking at income

- Are you booking the number of weeks that you anticipated?

- Is any particular part of the season proving difficult to book?

- Are you having trouble getting payments in from people?

Increasing bookings
Corrective action can include the following:

- taking out short-term advertising, for example in a newspaper – this can be expensive but is one of the few ways of getting a message out quickly if you have specific dates to sell;

- making sure that your local Tourist Information Centre knows about your vacancies – many run referral schemes. Join any local 'hotline' services that handle referrals;

- sharing information with local operators in the same business – think about referring business between yourselves;

- for late bookings, considering discounting as an incentive;

- if you have a website, posting late booking vacancies and special offers up on the front page;

- considering mailing regular customers with details of special offers and late booking availability;

- considering special promotions for off-peak weeks that are always harder to sell, and trying tie-ins to special days or events, for example Valentine's Day, or local festivals.

Improving cash flow into the business
- Is there any scope for changing your terms to obtain a larger deposit and earlier payment of the full amount (for new customers only)?

- Ensure that overdue amounts are promptly progressed.

Other income initiatives
Gauge how other operators in your sector and area are doing (but be aware that you may not get the full story from some people). If the general consensus is that you are one of the few having a bad season, then consider whether there is something more structural that needs looking at. Are your brochures doing a good job for you? Are your tariffs out of step with competitors? Are you spending enough on advertising?

Looking at expenditure

Analyse your expenditure forecasts. What is going wrong?

An analysis of your costs can help in deciding what corrective action, if any, you can take. You will be looking for:

- areas where you can make savings by reducing consumption – e.g. electricity, cleaning supplies – but without impacting adversely on customers;

- cheaper sources of supply;

- areas where you can defer spending, for example on major capital projects which can be put back;

- areas where you can cancel future spending plans;

- areas where you can do work yourself rather than paying someone else to do it.

But don't make false economies. Reducing advertising expenditure may save you money but reduce your potential income. Don't defer maintenance jobs that may become major work in the future. And you must make sure that standards are maintained: you want customers to come back and you won't do that by cutting corners.

If you are short of cash, investigate whether there are any local barter schemes in operation. Many areas now run LETS schemes (Local Employment Trading Schemes) which enable the trading of services between individuals. This can be well worth looking into if you think you have a marketable skill that you can trade for another skill that you can use in your business.

CHANGING PERSONAL CIRCUMSTANCES

Perhaps you or your family are not happy with the life you now lead. Perhaps a change of circumstances, illness for example, means that you cannot undertake the work you need to with resulting financial problems as costs escalate.

Whatever the reason, a change of personal circumstances may mean selling your business. This can take a long time: it is possible that it may take more than one season to sell a holiday letting complex. So be prepared for this – you may not have a quick or easy exit, unless you compromise on price.

Employing someone else to run the business can be an option, but only for larger operations. Most small businesses would not generate sufficient profit to justify this.

Some practical tips

- Make sure before you start that you understand the realities of what you are undertaking.

- Make sure before you start that your family understand and are committed to the business.

- Take out insurance to cover you against inability to work due to illness or accident.

- Make sure that there is family time which is not work-related. It is a common problem in small businesses that boundaries between work and office can become blurred.

ENJOYING SUCCESS

Hopefully, you will reach a stage where you have completed the renovations or restorations you undertook, you have built up a solid base of loyal customers and you feel that you have achieved what you set out to achieve.

But you can never really rest on your laurels:

- The maintenance of holiday lets goes on and on, and standards are increasing all the time.

- You can't guarantee that your loyal customers will carry on returning, for whatever reason, and so you should always be looking to attract new customers.

- Circumstances change and you must be prepared to embrace those changes.

- Technology changes, as we are seeing with the Internet, which will fundamentally change the way we do business.

- There are always things that can be improved.

But if you have built the business to a level that you are happy with, what do you do next?

- Do you continue running the business yourself? The challenge here is to keep motivated and interested season after season, changeover day after changeover day, so that standards are maintained.

- Do you increase the services you offer, perhaps expanding into a meals service, or short courses, for example?

- Do you expand? If you have the cash or the borrowing power, you may wish to consider either renovating another building or buying a property nearby. Beware of overstretching yourself, but this option can make sense as, for example, marketing four properties costs no more than marketing three.

● Do you let go? You could consider training up someone to take over if profits are large enough to cover an additional salary.

● Do you sell up? And then?

CASE STUDIES

Fiona and Michael take it easy

After five years, Fiona and Michael have built a successful, quality business. They have worked hard during that time, particularly to build their reputation as providers of specialist heritage breaks for the overseas market.

They have had little time off while doing this and now decide that they want to ease back a little. But neither of them want to sell up or to give up control of the special breaks side of the business that they have worked so hard to build. They decide to employ someone part-time to take over the day-to-day running of the business. They offer their smallest unit as rent-free accommodation for the manager, thereby always having someone on site in case of emergencies and allowing them to take more time off.

Fiona and Michael will retain control of marketing and organising special breaks and courses, as well as overseeing the property and making sure that standards are maintained. They advertise for a manager.

Sue decides to expand

Sue finds over the first few years of trading that her emphasis on high quality accommodation pays off. She made contacts with businesses in the area and now finds that most of her business comes from a local company who have a training school in the area – they use her flat to accommodate training staff who are on secondment for a month at a time.

Sue approaches the personnel officer of the company to see whether they could use any further accommodation and receives a favourable response. There is a house already divided into two flats close by Sue's home. Sue decides to take out a loan to buy the property and refurbish the flats. She plans to rent them primarily as holiday lets during the summer, adding the details to her existing website which generates most of her holiday let business, and to make the flats available to the company during the rest of the year, offering them bookings on a week-by-week basis.

George branches out

George has found that he enjoys the holiday let business more than he thought he would. He has found that people choosing to stay on his smallholding are genuinely interested in his animals and way of life, and always want to help out. In fact, many of his guests seem to be people who are thinking about setting up as smallholders themselves, or who have a dream of owning a piece of land and some animals sometime in the future.

George starts to think about whether he could offer hands-on, practical smallholding courses in the spring and autumn; he has the expertise to pass on to people and believes that he can communicate that experience to others. He knows he could advertise in specialist smallholders' magazines. This would be his only additional cost and so he decides to do some more research on demand and how much he could charge for these courses with a view to extending the length of his season.

CHECKLIST

● Diary a regular date to review progress.

● Keep your business plan updated.

● Don't be afraid to take action if you need to.

● Finally, think about what you're going to do next.

Further Reading

Legislation

Legislation Affecting Serviced and Self-catering Accommodation Businesses ('*The Pink Booklet*'), available from regional tourist boards or the English Tourism Council, Thames Tower, Black's Road, London W6 9EL. Tel. (0870) 606 72014. Website: *www.englishtourism.org.uk*

THE ENGLISH TOURISM COUNCIL

The ETC also provides various information sheets, regional tourism surveys and the following:

First Steps in Tourism
Signs for Tourism Businesses
Providing Accessible Accommodation
Quality Standard for Self-catering Accommodation in England

OTHER TOURISM PUBLICATIONS

Success with Farm-Based Tourist Accommodation
Success with Farm Diversification

Both available from MAFF Publications, Admail 6000, London SW1A 2AX. Tel: (0645) 335577.

BUSINESS MATTERS

Lloyds TSB Small Business Guide, Sara Williams (Penguin, 2000).
Preparing a Winning Business Plan, Matthew Record (How To Books, 2000).
Starting Your Own Business, Jim Green (How To Books, 2000)

The 'Which?' Guide to Starting Your Own Business, Jane Vass (Which? Books, 1999).

TAX AND NATIONAL INSURANCE

Among the many leaflets available from your local tax office:

Starting Your Own Business (pse1)
National Insurance Contributions for Self-Employed People Class 2 and 4 (CWL2)
National Insurance Contributions for Self-employed People with Low Earnings (CAO2)
Self Assessment – A Guide to Keeping Records for the Self-Employed (SA/BK3)
First Steps as a New Employer (NE1)

Useful Addresses

BUILDING WORKS, ARCHITECTS AND SURVEYORS

Association of Plumbing and Heating Contractors, 14–15 Ensign House, Ensign Business Centre, Westwood Way, Coventry CV4 8JA. Tel: (024) 7647 0626.

The Council for Registered Gas Installers (CORGI), 1 Elmwood, Chineham Business Park, Crockford Lane, Basingstoke, Hampshire RG24 8WG. Tel: (01256) 372300.

Electrical Contractors' Association, 34 Palace Court, London W2 4HY. Tel: (020) 7229 1266.

Federation of Master Builders, Gordon Fisher House, 14–15 Great James Street, London WC1N 3DP. Tel: (020) 7242 7583.

National Federation of Builders, Construction House, 56–64 Leonard Street, London EC2A 4JX. Tel: (020) 7608 5150.

National Inspection Council for Electrical Installation Contracting, Vintage House, 37 Albert Embankment, London SE1 7UJ. Tel: (020) 7564 2323.

Royal Institute of British Architects, 66 Portland Place, London W1N 4AD. Tel: (020) 7303 3700.

Royal Institution of Chartered Surveyors, 12 Great George Street, Parliament Square, London SW1P 3AD. Tel: (020) 7222 7000.

FINANCE AND INSURANCE

Association of Chartered Certified Accountants, 29 Lincolns Inn Fields, London WC2A 3EE. Tel: (020) 7242 6855. *Website: www.acca.co.uk*

British Insurance and Investment Brokers' Association, BIIBA House, 14 Bevis Marks, London EC3A 7NT. Tel: (020) 7623 9043.

Inland Revenue – Contact your local tax office. For self-assessment queries tel: (0645) 000444. For the Helpline for New Employers tel: (0845) 6070143. *Website: www.inlandrevenue.gov.uk*

Institute of Chartered Accountants in England and Wales, PO Box 433, Chartered Accountants' Hall, Moorgate Place, London EC2P 2BJ. Tel: (020) 7920 8100. *Website: www.icaew.co.uk*

Institute of Insurance Brokers, Higham Business Centre, Midland Road, Higham Ferrers, Northamptonshire NN10 8DW. Tel: (01933) 410003.

BUSINESS ORGANISATIONS

Association of British Chambers of Commerce, Manning House, 22 Carlisle Place, London SW1P 1JA. Tel: (020) 7565 2000. *Website: www.britishchambers.org.uk*

Federation of Small Businesses, Whittle Way, Blackpool, Lancashire FY4 2FE. Tel: (01253) 336000. *Website: www.fsb.org.uk*

NATIONAL TOURIST BOARDS

British Tourist Authority, Thames Tower, Black's Road, London W6 9EL. Tel: (020) 8563 3186. *Website: www.tourismtrade.org.uk*

Northern Ireland Tourist Board, St Anne's Court, 59 North Street, Belfast BT1 1NB. Tel: (028) 9023 1221. *Website: www.ni-tourism.com*

Wales Tourist Board, Brunel House, 2 Fitzalan Road, Cardiff CF24 0UY. Tel: (029) 2047 5291. *Website: www.visitwales.com*

REGIONAL TOURIST BOARDS

Cumbria Tourist Board, Ashleigh, Holly Road, Windermere, Cumbria LA23 2AQ. Tel: (015394) 444444.

East of England Tourist Board, Toppesfield Hall, Hadleigh, Suffolk IP7 5DN. Tel: (01473) 822922.

Heart of England Tourist Board, Larkhill, Worcester WR5 2EZ. Tel: (01905) 761100.

London Tourist Board, 6th Floor, Glen House, Stag Place, London SW1E 5LT. Tel: (020) 7932 2000.

Northumbria Tourist Board, Aykley Heads, Durham, DH1 5UX. Tel: (0191) 3753000.

North West Tourist Board, Swan House, Swan Meadow Road, Wigan Pier, Wigan WN3 5BB. Tel: (01942) 821222.

South East England Tourist Board, The Old Brew House, Warwick Park, Tunbridge Wells, Kent TN2 5TU. Tel: (01892) 540766.

Southern Tourist Board, 40 Chamberlayne Road, Eastleigh, Hampshire SO5 5JH. Tel: (0238) 0620006.

South West Tourism, Woodwater Park, Exeter, EX2 5WT. Tel: (0870) 4420830.

Yorkshire Tourist Board, 312 Tadcaster Road, York YO2 2HF. Tel: (01904) 707961.

OTHER

Business Link Helpline. Tel: (08456) 045678. *www.business adviceonline.org.* Can direct you to your local Business Link office.

Department of Trade and Industry Enquiry Unit, 1 Victoria Street, London SW1H 0ET. Tel: (020) 7215 5000. *Website: www.dti.gov.uk*

Department of Trade and Industry Publications Orderline, Admail 528, London SW1W 8YT. Tel: (0870) 1502500.

Health and Safety Executive Gas Safety Advice Line. Tel: (0800) 300363.

Health and Safety Executive Infoline. Tel: (0541) 545500. *Website: www.open.gov.uk/hse*

Health and Safety Executive Information Centre, Broad Lane, Sheffield S3 7HQ. Fax: (0114) 2892333. For written or fax queries only.

HM Customs & Excise – For VAT advice, contact your nearest VAT Business Advice Centre, address in local telephone directories. *Website: www.hmce.gov.uk*

LETSlink UK, 2 Kent Street, Portsmouth, Hampshire PO1 3BS. Tel: (01705) 730639. For information on local LETS schemes.

The Office of the Data Protection Registrar, Wycliffe House, Water Lane, Wilmslow, Cheshire SK9 5AF. Tel: 01625 545745. *Website: www.dataprotection.gov.uk*

The Office of Gas and Electricity Markets, 130 Whitton Road, London SW1V 1LQ. Tel: (0800) 887777.

Rural Development Commission, 141 Castle Street, Salisbury, Wiltshire SP1 3TP. Tel: (01722) 336255.

The Stationery Office Ltd, 51 Nine Elms Lane, London SW8 5DR. Tel: (0870) 2422345. For HMSO publications.

TV Licensing (Hotel Section), Bond Street, Bristol BS98 1TL. Tel: (0117) 9219321. For hotel comprehensive TV licences.

Index

Printed in Great Britain
by Amazon

45192075R00075